Open Innovation Essentials for Small and Medium Enterprises

Open Innovation Essentials for Small and Medium Enterprises

A Guide to Help Entrepreneurs in Adopting the Open Innovation Paradigm in Their Business

Luca Escoffier, Adriano La Vopa, Phyllis Speser, and Daniel Satinsky

BEP BUSINESS EXPERT PRESS

Open Innovation Essentials for Small and Medium Enterprises: A Guide to Help Entrepreneurs in Adopting the Open Innovation Paradigm in Their Business

First published in 2016 by
Business Expert Press, LLC
222 East 46th Street, New York, NY 10017
www.businessexpertpress.com

ISBN-13: 978-1-63157-242-5 (paperback)
ISBN-13: 978-1-63157-243-2 (e-book)

Business Expert Press Entrepreneurship and Small Business Management Collection

Collection ISSN: 1946-5653 (print)
Collection ISSN: 1946-5661 (electronic)

Cover and interior design by Exeter Premedia Services Private Ltd., Chennai, India

First edition: 2016

10 9 8 7 6 5 4 3 2 1

Printed in the United States of America.

Abstract

Small and medium enterprises (SMEs) have to approach open innovation differently than large companies. *Open Innovation Essentials for Small and Medium Enterprises* provides the first comprehensive introduction to the practice of open innovation expressly for entrepreneurs and managers of SMEs. The authors provide strategies, techniques, and "tricks of the trade" that enable SMEs to establish and operate open innovation systems that increase their business's profitability and enhance the long-term value of their equity. They explain how SMEs can use open innovation to develop and sell products and services or to acquire, mature, and sell technology and intellectual property rights. Tools such as brokers, auctions, crowdsourcing, technology transfer, and spin-ups are presented in ways that make it easy to use them in your own company. The entire book can be read on an airplane flight or in an evening, making it useful for people already in business and faculty or students seeking supplemental reading material for courses.

Keywords

business acceleration, crowdsourcing, intellectual property (IP), IP auctions, IP brokerage, open innovation, small and medium enterprises (SMEs), spin-up companies, technology transfer

Contents

About the Contributors

Luca Escoffier graduated in law from the University of Parma, Italy, in 2001. He then earned a Master of Laws in Intellectual Property Law in 2003 (World Intellectual Property Organization [WIPO]). After some years spent in law firms and in an Italian nano-biotech company, he moved to Seattle in 2008 to work as a visiting lecturer at the University of Washington where he also earned a certificate in business administration from the Foster Business School (2010). Between 2008 and 2010, he was one of the editors of the RCLIP IP precedent database, the largest collection of Asian intellectual property (IP) cases in the world. He has been a fellow of the Stanford-Vienna Transatlantic Technology Law Forum since 2006. He was one of the four experts in IP law who had been selected as fellows of the Institute of Intellectual Property in Tokyo in 2009 to write a report on knowledge transfer activities in Europe and Japan, and in 2014, one of the Minerva fellows at the EU-Japan Centre for Industrial Cooperation (Tokyo) tasked with the drafting of a detailed analysis of the Japanese technology transfer system and about the challenges and opportunities for European small and medium enterprises (SMEs). Mr. Escoffier is a Singularity University alumnus (GSP10), and from 2010, he has been working as an external licensing manager for the University of Trieste, Italy, and as CEO of Usque Ad Sidera LLC (Seattle). Since 2011, he has been the CIO and then advisor to Qurami (Rome), a leading Italian start-up involved in the time-saving business, and from 2012, one of the cofounders of Impact HUB Trieste, Italy, a coworking space and accelerator based in Italy, which fosters social innovation. In 2014, he cofounded Innoventually (Italy), a one-stop source for innovation (and first open innovation-focused Italian company) where every step of the innovation path is handled either by Innoventually or by one of the partners operating from three different continents. Having worked for companies, as cofounder, CEO, consultant, and for universities as licensing manager, and as a scholar in three continents, Luca Escoffier is widely recognized as one of the most knowledgeable tech transfer experts from Italy. Mr. Escoffier is also the Project Manager of a new Tech Transfer Helpdesk that will be launched from 2016 by the EU-Japan Centre for Industrial Cooperation in Tokyo. Beside being the author of several dozens of articles on IP and technology transfer, he is also the coauthor and coeditor of *Nanotechnology Commercialization for Managers and Scientists* (Pan Stanford Publishing, 2012), and *Commercializing Nanomedicine: Industrial Applications, Patents, and Ethics* (Pan Stanford Publishing, 2015).

Adriano La Vopa is a physicist with an International Master in Nanotechnologies (IMN). He worked in a scientific park as leader of innovative projects based on technology transfer of new materials and technologies, mainly consulting Italian enterprises. He managed a start-up involved in amorphous metal casting, a technology transferred from the space sector, as technical business development and production manager. He worked as consultant, partnering with several consultancies, mainly focusing on technology transfer and brokerage; his clients were mainly SMEs seeking to improve their competitiveness by means of innovation and new technology acquisition and implementation. He has been a regulatory affairs manager for LG Electronics, representing the company at the main discussion tables of consumer electronics trade associations and at the European Commission. He is currently employed at Philips where he works in different innovation domains, helping teams in adopting open innovation and its tools.

Phyllis (Phyl) Speser is a founder and CEO of Foresight Science & Technology, a global consultancy in technology transfer, commercialization, and intellectual asset management and supply chain formation with offices in the United States, Great Britain, Chile, and Singapore. She is the author of the best-selling textbook *The Art and Science of Technology Transfer* (John Wiley and Sons, 2006) and has supported commercialization of technologies across the breadth of science and technology, working for major corporations, SMEs, universities, government agencies, foundations, and research institutes around the globe. During her career of over 35 years, she has taught intellectual property at the SUNY Buffalo Law School, political science at the Universität Mannheim (Germany) and SUNY Buffalo, and archaeology at The American University in Washington, DC; been a multiple federal research and development (R&D) award winner on projects involving artificial intelligence and other advanced methods applied to problems of transitioning and commercialization technology; and a lobbyist (Small Business Innovation Research, Small Business Technology Transfer Research, Stevenson-Wydler amendments, Archaeological Resources Protection Act amendments, point on federal budget for the science community for 10 years, and other legislation and related regulations). She also has been instrumental in the development of technology transfer programs such as the New York State Centers of Excellence as an advisor to Governor Hugh Carey. Dr. Speser is a member of the Bar Association of the District of Columbia, the Association of University Technology Managers (where she was a vice president and member of the board of directors), the Licensing Executives Society (where she was chair, Strategic Alliance Committee), and a member of the Association of European Science and Technology Transfer Professionals. She served two terms on the Board of the Technology Transfer Society and is a recipient of that Society's Certificate of Appreciation (1991). She also was chairman of its Task Force on National Technology Transfer Policy (1989–1991), and received Best Paper, Annual Meeting (1987). She was a gubernatorial appointment to the Board of the Washington Technology Center from 1994 to 1997. Her PhD and JD, cum laude, are from the State University of New York at Buffalo, and she holds a Registered Technology Transfer Professional certification from the Alliance of Technology Transfer Professionals. She is a recipient of the Rhododendron Award from the school districts of Port Townsend, Washington, and Mendocino, California, for work in science education and is a founder of the Northwest Natural Resources Group, a foundation supporting sustainable forestry.

Daniel Satinsky is the vice president for business development at Foresight Science & Technology. Among his responsibilities for the company, he leads Foresight's activities in development (spinning up) and sale of small R&D companies that are based on university, research hospital, government, and nonprofit lab early-stage technologies. He has been instrumental in the initiation and development of three start-up companies and has acted as a business development and market entry consultant to a number of established companies. He has been particularly active in innovation and technology transfer in the Russian xiiABOUT THE CONTRIBUTORS

Federation. He is a recognized authority on the Russian business environment, particularly on efforts there to build the knowledge-based technology sector. He has authored or coauthored innovation-related articles published by the Woodrow Wilson Center Press, The New York Academy of Sciences, World Trade Executive, and the *Thunderbird International Business Review*. Mr. Satinsky holds a BA (summa cum laude) from Michigan State University's James Madison College, a juris doctor degree from Northeastern University Law School, and a Master of Law and Diplomacy degree from the Fletcher School of Law and Diplomacy. For more than 10 years, he served as the president of the board of the U.S.-Russia Chamber of Commerce of New England. In addition, he is a member of the Massachusetts Bar Association, a member of the Boston Committee on Foreign Relations, and an associate of the Davis Center for Russian and Eurasian Studies at Harvard University.

Acknowledgments

This book has been written by four different coauthors, who all have put their own work, expertise, and knowledge into words that we hope will usefully guide readers through the exciting experience of running a business. In doing so, we have also taken some interesting tips from different sources.

Therefore, we would like to thank:

Ross Dowson, who gave us the possibility to use his crowdsourcing landscape.

Innoventually's folks who provided some interesting suggestions on challenges, how to run them, and how to engage with a crowd, as well as some important ones on how to monetize IP rights.

Foresight's thousands of entrepreneurial clients who are adapting scientific research into new products or services and the Foresight staff of experts providing the commercial insight to these entrepreneurs that we have capsulized in our chapters for this book.

CHAPTER 1

Introduction

Open Innovation for Small and Medium-Sized Enterprises

Phyllis Speser, JD, PhD, RTTP, and Adriano La Vopa

This book is about how small and midsized companies can make money by leveraging the intellectual assets and intellectual property (IP) of others. In today's global competition, using external sources and resources for innovation makes sound business sense, no matter what size the company. Up until now, however, most practical guides to open innovation have focused on what large companies should do. While there is a lot of overlap, small and midsized companies face different challenges and opportunities in developing, commercializing, and selling innovations—and thus how they practice open innovation should be correspondingly different.

In this book, we illustrate how open innovation can be effectively and profitably used by small and medium enterprises (SMEs). It is primarily written for managers, entrepreneurs, owners, and investors seeing to increase profitability associated with new product development. It will also be helpful for students and other people interested in a practical look at this aspect of the global "innovation economy."

We believe this book is particularly timely. There is a glut of good technology on the global market today—a condition that most observers agree will last another decade or two. It is a great time to be a "buyer" (which includes licensee) of IP and technology because it is a buyer's market. What we show you is how to think about open innovation and where, and how, it makes money in ways that increase your net profit on the income statement and company value on the balance sheet. Please let us know how well we have done that by e-mailing us at phyl.speser@ foresightst.com, adrianolavopa@hotmail.com.

What Is Open Innovation?

Since its birth back in 2003, *open innovation* has been a hot topic of discussion. By googling these two simple words, one can easily retrieve more than 86 million of results in half a second, which demonstrates the "buzziness" of the paradigm.

Open innovation has become a kind of umbrella that embraces lots of different practices and methods. Despite the diversity, one key concept runs throughout: Open innovation means opening up the boundaries of an organization and collaborating with others on the outside to share ideas and knowledge and to acquire IP rights in technologies and know-how in order to bring new products to market more profitably.

In the rest of this introduction, we provide a conceptual framework for thinking about open innovation at SMEs. The context for this framework is how companies manage their idea flow, now that external sources are as important as internal ones for bringing new process and product technologies to market.

A useful construct for discussing idea flow is the innovation funnel. The innovation funnel is basically a set of steps to be followed to bring an idea to launch. By launch we mean developing and making available a new service, product, production method, or other useful things.

The management of the funnel is subject to various theories for optimizing it. Some of these theories even have given rise to software implementations that can be used to manage the flow of innovations from idea to something accessible by others. Figure 1.1 is a visual depiction of the innovation funnel. Included are what are commonly seen as major steps and control points (e.g., *gates*, or *milestones* in the lingo of project managers). Control points ensure one step only ends after certain deliverables are provided. The deliverables open the gate for the next step to begin. Of course, the approach in the picture is not intended to be the only possible implementation of an innovation funnel. Funnels need to

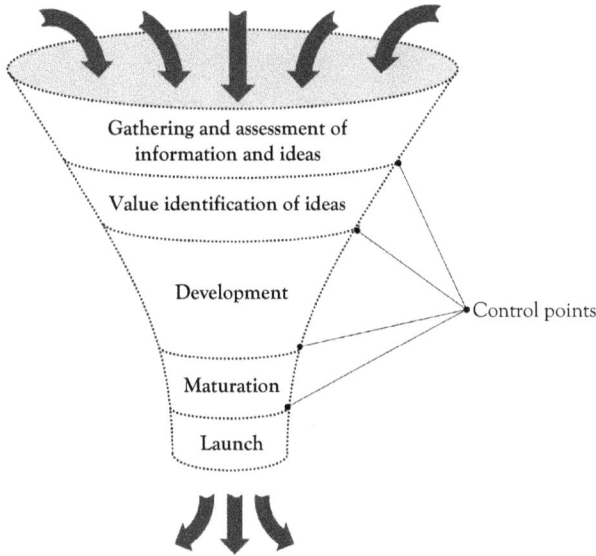

Figure 1.1 The innovation funnel

be customized according to each SME's needs and processes. To use an old adage, "*One size does not fit all.*"

The use of the term *open innovation* was developed as a counter-concept to *closed innovation* (Figure 1.2) by Henry Chesbrough of Harvard University. Chesbrough coined the term open innovation in the book of the same name, although he was building on a body of literature that went back to the 1960s. He contrasted open innovation with closed innovation, which was a common business practice in the economic boom years after World War II (WWII) and up to the Vietnam War. The rebuilding of global economies after WWII provided a rising tide in which many boats floated. In closed innovation, the lessons of secrecy for successful military weapons development were reflected in the paradigm for corporate research and development (R&D) and new product development.

Innovation is closed when the organization does everything within its own walls without disclosing anything outside except after the IP is protected and secured. Confidentiality and noncompete agreements and a culture of secrecy existed in which R&D and new product development was controlled and occurred within the "walls" of companies.

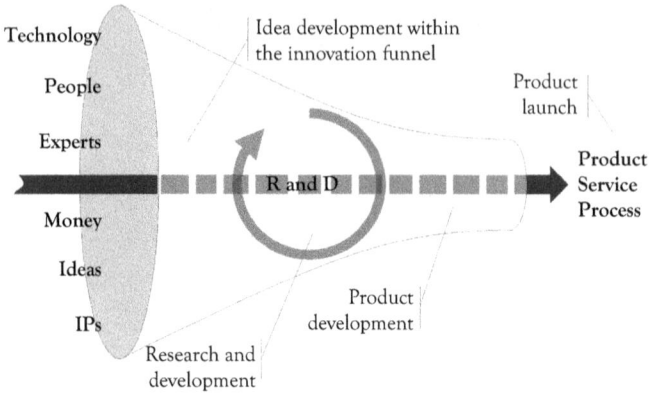

Figure 1.2 Closed innovation model

In this paradigm, the key to success was to hire the best brains possible under labor contracts that specified full control over labor conditions and stated that the output of their invention and innovation belonged to the employer.

This way of doing business is associated with the syndrome of "not invented here" (NIH). In one of the first analysis of this syndrome, by Kats and Allen back in 1982, the authors made it clear that such behavior inhibits innovating effectively. At the very beginning of their paper, the NIH syndrome is described as "the tendency of a project group of stable composition to believe it possesses the monopoly of knowledge of its field, which leads it to reject new ideas from outsiders to the likely detriment of its performance." This definition is important because it summarizes the mindset that the R&D groups of most corporate, government, and non-profit institutes used to have in the past. Even today, especially where the culture of innovation is not particularly ingrained, this syndrome can be a cause of poor growth by a company. Following common practice, we will call the mindset of NIH the "silo mindset" (Figure 1.3). Silos create walls within the same organization and between it and others, which prevent sharing ideas, knowledge, technology, and know-how.

When the individual has the NIH syndrome, he or she is not prone to learn and share. There is a high possibility that useful knowledge that both that person and others discover will be frozen. Indeed, with the silo mindset, sharing is not considered an option. The potential range

No knowledge sharing

Dep. A   Dep. B   Dep. C   Outsider

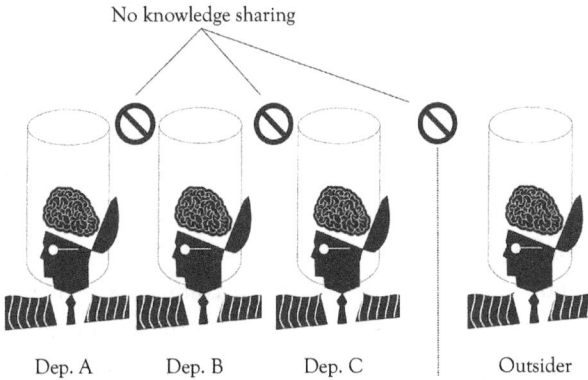

Figure 1.3 Closed silo mindset

of realizations and applications for an idea is limited by what is known inside the walls of the lab where the inventor is employed and by the knowledge of the few people to whom it has been disclosed. While an NIH mindset may have made sense in the age before telephones and the Internet, when knowledge was often *de facto* localized and territorial, it was doomed to short-circuit company success with the emergence of Internet- and cellular-based instant and ubiquitous electronic communications. Easy access to both real-time and asynchronous communication meant the ways professionals, researchers, engineers, managers, sales staff, service staff, customers, and vendors connected began evolving rapidly.

Diverse factors have contributed to the crumbling of the "closed innovation." The Internet with its social networking, easier global travel, and the loss of lifelong job security at a time of increased geographic mobility are a few examples. But such factors were secondary to the impact of closed walls and the silo mindset on younger employees and the students who were tomorrow's employees. Unable to express their full potentials within 1950s-style organizations, the creative power, innovative brains, and venturesome spirits of the baby boomers and Generation Xers bumped up against "bureaucracy." Enough smart people quit their jobs or school and started their own business based on the ideas, knowledge, and gumption that a new start-up culture had emerged whose heroes were people like Bill Gates (Microsoft), Herbert Boyer (Genetech), and Mark Zuckerberg (Facebook). They became wealthy and leaders in their markets through innovation. This dispersion of creativity and knowledge into start-ups created the humus out of which the open innovation paradigm grew. The rise of high-tech start-ups presented established big companies broader opportunities to source and benefit from outside innovation. Unlike most university technology, the technology from start-ups was more mature and thus had shorter lead times to market. The more technology there was to license—especially technology mature enough to be ready for market—the more it made business sense to acquire and use it. This wealth of outside technology encouraged companies to reinvent their business models for R&D and product development by opening their doors to external collaborations and intellectual asset and IP acquisitions. Outside ideas, knowledge, technologies, know-how, innovative people, and access to risk capital became tools for successful product innovation and the growth it can bring.

The open innovation paradigm was a consequence of such transformations. In roughly 25 years, the paradigm of R&D and product development has changed from closed to open innovation (Figure 1.4). The management of the innovation funnel has changed forever.

The open innovation paradigm, like closed innovation, is associated with a mindset, this time, "proudly found elsewhere" (PFE). PFE was presented in an article from two Proctor & Gamble (P&G) employees in 2006. Their new innovation model involved "educating" their internal R&D departments in how to find innovations elsewhere and being proud

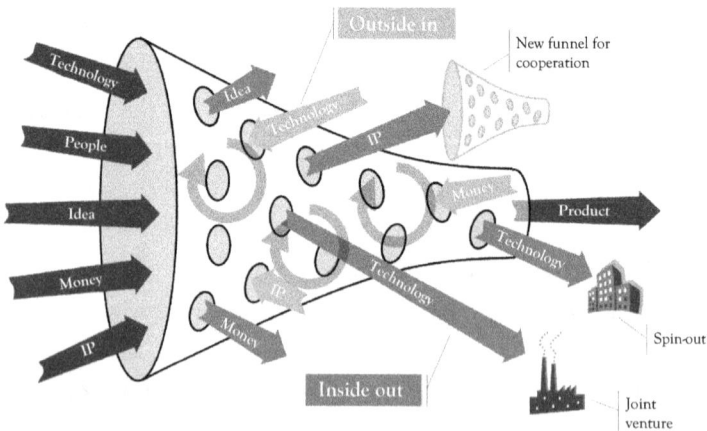

Figure 1.4 Open innovation

Sharing of knowledge

OPEN MINDSET

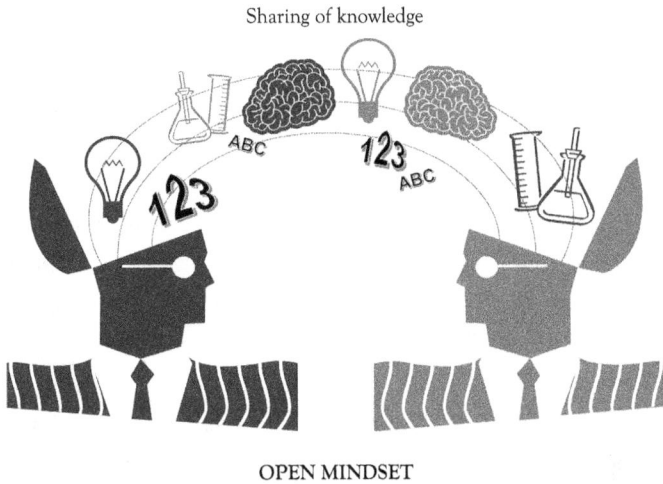

Figure 1.5 Open mindset. When the mindset is open, there is an opportunity for exchanging more knowledge

of doing so. One sentence of their article summed up the business case for open innovation: "For every P&G researcher there were 200 scientists or engineers elsewhere in the world who were just as good—a total of perhaps 1.5 million people whose talents we could potentially use." It is clear that this approach meant a radical change in the way their company innovated and the mindset of employees involved in R&D and new product development (Figure 1.5).

The open approach, and the open innovation in general, created a different way of exploiting the immense resources outside the company. Open innovators are merchants of intellectual assets and IP. Their mindset endorses exporting and importing those resources via *inside-out* and the *outside-in* knowledge sharing and transactions (also shown in Figure 1.4). Large companies were among the first adopters, as in the past century, the Internet infrastructure and methods for finding and acquiring external intellectual assets and property were immature. Only larger firms could afford corporate technology scouts to walk the exhibit halls and meeting rooms of professional and trade association meetings.

Of course, the inside-out practice is not new to most of the universities, research hospitals, and research institutions. Indeed, it has been quite common for larger organizations to use licensing, sale, or donation of patents they never have used or were no longer using and which were no longer relevant to the organization's plans for the future. This practice was used not only by corporations but also became well established at universities, government labs, and other research organizations. Whenever one hears about technology transfer, technology brokerage, licensing, IP trading, or any other similar term, it is likely that the seller (or donor) is addressing the inside-out practice. However, as explained in Chesbrough's book, open innovation goes beyond practices focused on surplus intellectual assets or IP. Open innovation is focused on the bottom line. In open innovation, inside-out transfers go beyond surplus to potentially include any sharing, selling, licensing, or loaning of inside knowledge, know-how, and technologies. Any innovation is a candidate for being combined with expertise and risk capital to create new opportunities for bigger profits.

The big shift in corporate paradigms, which led to open innovation, occurred when larger companies began embracing outside-in. Bill Joy, cofounder of Sun Microsystems, used to say: "No matter who you are, most of the smartest people work for someone else." This illuminating sentence summarizes the essence of the outside-in approach. It is an approach now commonplace for multinational corporations and for agile SMEs. It means an organization is sourcing its "missing knowledge" from the outside world, looking into different domains and arenas for intellectual assets available for sharing and IP to buy. It can be passive or proactive, as when an entity goes live with broadcast challenges either on its own website and through its network or via open innovation intermediaries. Open innovation need not be restricted to companies either. For example, the Harvard Medical School launched a challenge for gathering new ideas on Type 1 diabetes research. This challenge resulted in 190 submissions from different members of Harvard's community, and 12 of them were selected as pioneering ideas to be developed in proper research projects. It is interesting to note that some of the winners were not experts. Some of the winners were still undergraduate students or patients. It is important to note that, because in open innovation the sourced idea is more important than the source itself. P&G Connect + Develop portal is an example related to for-profits. Through this portal, P&G calls for inventors, other companies, and individuals to submit their innovative proposals to them. Those ideas are assessed and evaluated by their internal employees, and if a match is found, the submitter is encouraged to work with P&G to further develop the idea to bring it to life.

A unique type of outside-in open innovation is *crowdsourcing*. This term applies to any practice that sources ideas, knowledge, or technology from a defined crowd of people (e.g., experts, companies, individuals, users' communities, etc.), which can include the public in general. In Figure 1.6 are some examples of crowdsourcing platforms and providers, divided into domains of offered services: marketplaces, platforms, media and content, ventures, and product markets.

Being open to innovation means, then, being willing to allow new sources of knowledge, information, and resources cross the walls of the organization, whether it is out in or in out. It means collaborating with the external world and using what is outside of the organization in order to attain greater SME short-, mid-, and (or) long-term profitability. Open innovation practices create a higher number of opportunities, avoid "reinventing the wheel," and leverage the achievements and failures of others. The scholarly literature is full of dissertations and case studies (Apple, Intel, Hewlett Packard, Xerox, P&G, Philips, etc.). In this book, we mine that literature and our experiences as practitioners of open innovation to provide some practical and essential methods, as well as clear guidelines on how to use open innovation in SMEs.

When Does It Make Sense to Practice Open Innovation?

For SMEs, it makes no sense to get involved in open innovation unless you are going to make more money doing it than you would not doing it. Whether the product you hope to sell is a knickknack or something that will feed the hungry, clothe the naked, house the homeless, heal the sick, bring energy to cities and clean water to the deserts, and do all that at the same time, companies still have to make money or they will go out of business. Open innovation works when it gets you novelties more cheaply than other alternatives or gets you new products or services, where IP protection enables charging monopoly prices. In short, it gets you increased net revenues. As David Speser, cofounder of Foresight Science & Technology, says, "Without sales, companies die."

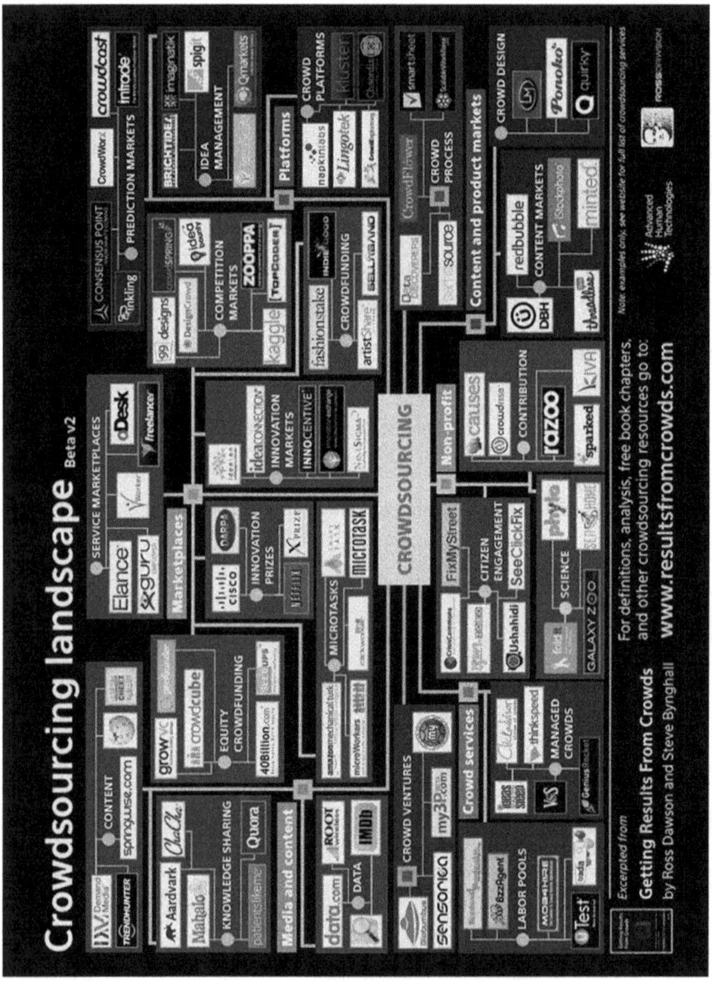

Figure 1.6 Crowdsourcing landscape

Net Revenues – Cost of Goods Sold = Gross Profit

Revenues need to be considered in light of expenses. The next item in determining if practicing open innovation makes sense is the cost of goods sold. Costs in open innovation include expenses for finding ideas and technologies, doing due diligence on them, using or acquiring them, and productizing them (or incorporating it in another product or adapting it to use when making, selling, or supporting products). If IP is involved, it also involves layers and filing fees for obtaining and maintaining those rights, monitoring for infringement, and enforcing those rights against infringers. The best-case open innovation scenario is you "buy" ideas or technologies that allow you to get a product or service that

- Is in high demand;
- Is IP protected; and
- Can be competitively priced and still make you a good profit.

When you own IP, it means that a group of intellectual assets is protected. Protected means you have a legal monopoly to exploit your product for the life of the patent, copyright, or mask. The know-how you develop can be protected through trade secrets, enhancing your ability to execute better and thus discourage infringement by copying or stealing. Good trade and service marks can provide additional protection if customers associate your mark with that type of goods.

On top of all this is the fact that your company, in the best-case scenario, gets to market ahead of your competitors. We call that having the first mover advantage. First mover advantage gives you a de facto monopoly on top of any IP-driven monopoly—at least until the competition responds.

Costs of Goods Sold (TIME 2) < Costs of Goods Sold (TIME 1)

It also means you have learning curve advantages. As you are already making, selling, and supporting the product, your company is figuring out the "tricks of the trade" ahead of others. The company is also able to respond to the market by improving the product and adding on tag-alongs like service and training contracts, warrantees, and consumables used with the product.

SMEs practicing open innovation often can drive down costs further by accessing government or foundation money. Around the world, local, regional, national, and multinational governments and nongovernmental organizations (NGOs) have money available to help acquire, further develop, and commercialize technology as part of economic development or human health and welfare initiatives. Winning government contracts and grants drives down the costs of goods sold as they subsidize those expenses. Where internal development of a technology is an option, conducting cooperative research and development with a government lab, university, nonprofit institute, or other company is another way to reduce costs.

Net Revenues From IP (TIME 2) – Cost of Goods Sold due to IP (TIME 2) > Net Revenues From IP – Costs of Goods Sold due to IP (TIME 1)

The icing on the cake in the best-case scenario is you license the IP rights for noncompetitive uses. You can also license it to competitors when the competitive advantage the IP formerly gave is no longer there. You might also license it to competitors if you know they are starting to work on competing technology. One increasingly used response is to make money off the competitors from royalty and fee payments to offset the reduction in revenues anticipated when they introduce their product. As revenues go down, your own costs usually do too. The result is a net profit so long as royalty and fee payments exceed IP maintenance fees and the costs of monitoring for, and preventing, infringement.

$\sum t$Net Revenues (Product Contribution + Royalties and Fees) – $\sum t$Cost of Goods Sold (Obtaining IP + Developing and Productizing IP + Maintaining IP + Enforcing IP) = $\sum$Gross Profit From IP

$\sum$Gross Profit × Discount Factor = Discounted Gross Profit From IP

We end up here: Open innovation makes sense when it creates a gross profit that, after discounting, meets your company's hurdle rate for investment of company money. Essentially, you only acquire a technology from outside where you can make a good profit off it.

Amortized IP (TIME 2) > Amortized IP (TIME 1)

In open innovation, there is often another plus. The value of the company, and thus its stock, goes up. As the IP is productized and contributes to sales revenues, its value on the balance sheet goes up. That bumps up intangible assets, which in turn bumps up total assets. Increases in total assets increase (without offsetting liabilities) the value of a company's stock.

Goodwill (TIME 2) > Goodwill (TIME 1)

Goodwill is another intangible asset. Product success generates goodwill for companies. So does a reputation for great technology and innovation. In open innovation, this intangible can bump up the value of goodwill. Where goodwill comes into play, the bump will be multiplied if the product heals the sick, feeds the hungry, brings water to the desert, makes clean energy, reduces pollution, or some other thing everyone agrees is a good thing. After all, doing good things usually generates goodwill.

Price Stock + Stock Options Price (TIME 2) > Price Stock + Stock Options Price (TIME 1)

Acquiring intellectual assets and IP relevant for the business contributes to stock price in two ways. First, the cost of acquisition (which is its current market price) now increases the value of the company's intangible assets. In the best-case scenario, the assets are up and the liabilities stable or down. The value of the stock goes up. The company can raise money by selling stock. As the price of stock goes up, less stock needs to be sold to raise the same amount of money.

In the best-case scenario, the IP will be very significant for the company. If it is, it is likely for some period there will be increased volatility in the stock price until the stock market settles on the value impact of the IP and related assets. Since volatility is an input when determining the value of a stock option and higher volatility drives up option prices, open innovation means a company can sell fewer stock options to raise the same amount of money than it would have had to sell without open innovation. If government regulations allow and it makes business sense, it can also buy back its options when volatility is lower and the price has settled.

Like any corporate practice, open innovation works when the net profits on the income statement and the value of company stock increase. This book provides SMEs with an overview on open innovation at SMEs and a set of tools to use in their innovation processes in order to increase profits and enhance the value of company stock.

The Chapters

The book has six chapters.

In Chapter 2, we focus on the use of brokers and auctions. Every SME has two choices in practicing open innovation: Do everything yourself or get help from vendors selling services that support open innovation. In this chapter, we look at some ways to address how to think about that choice and some tools to use, whichever the choice. This chapter also introduces you to the wealth of free web portals that have sprung up to help you find technologies that may be of interest.

Chapter 3 addresses technology transfer, which involves working with representatives from universities, research hospitals, government laboratories, and nonprofit research and development institutions to acquire technology. Technology transfer is now a mature field, and these kinds of public institutions have dedicated professionals to help you find and license the technology they have invented. Technology transfer works best when you have at least a rough idea of what you are looking for. As the technology invested by these institutions tends to be relatively immature, technology transfer works best for SMEs that have in-house capabilities in R&D and product development or access to these skills and capabilities.

Chapter 4 looks at crowdsolving (also called crowd sourcing), one of the newer approaches to open innovation. Crowdsolving can be an effective and cost-efficient tool for SMEs. It leverages the power of the web for finding new products or product enhancements and the technology for making and creating them. It is also a tool for selling or licensing technology.

Chapter 5 rounds out our discussion by presenting the spin-up business model. Spin-up involves in-licensing an immature technology and then out-licensing a "market-ready" technology or product. Almost every country today has subsidies available for developing technology intensive products and services. Much of this funding is only available to SMEs.

We conclude in Chapter 6 with a brief discussion on open innovation strategies for SMEs that leverage the approaches and tools in the earlier chapters to make you more money and greater profit.

CHAPTER 2

IP Brokerage and
IP Auctions

How an SME Can Benefit From
These Business Models

Luca Escoffier

Introduction

Among the different business models for open innovation, IP brokerage and IP auctions have become increasingly popular. These two business models can be profitably leveraged by small and medium enterprises (SMEs) for open innovation. In this chapter,[1] we explain why and offer some tips on how to use them. We use the term "IP" to mean intellectual property, which includes patents, copyrights, trademarks, trade secrets, and so forth. Usually, the most common rights being involved in brokering or auctions are those concerning registered IP.

In the IP brokerage model, an external agent, the IP broker, evaluates, values, and obtains a set of IP rights, usually from the original sources (e.g., an individual inventor or university or research center). The broker then licenses or sells these rights—either exclusively or nonexclusively— to other individuals or entities who can make use of them. What makes brokering particularly relevant for SMEs is the fact that prices for these portfolios have fallen. One reason is, the IP portfolio market has slowed in reaction to the Great Recession and the weaker global economy, especially

---

[1] Opinions expressed in this chapter are those of the author only. Nothing in this chapter can or should be interpreted as legal advice.

in the software field. Another factor is more jurisdictions are questioning the validity of software-related patents. In effect, there has been a market adjustment; so the "bubble" period is over (at least for the near term) and prices in general have reached some sort of stability. Like any vendor with excess inventory, brokers have greater incentives to sell portfolios they have accumulated as they can no longer assume prices for them will continue to rise on the one hand, and they still have to pay maintenance fees on the other.

This situation can make brokered portfolios affordable for SMEs. What we provide in this chapter is a strategy based on going out and seeking relevant technologies managed by brokers rather than waiting for a broker to approach you with an offer to sell rights to technology. A switch from the "push" to the "pull" approach allows the SME to aggregate technologies immediately relevant for the SME—either by acquiring a complete portfolio or by breaking it apart and only acquiring the IP of interest.

In the IP auction model, a broker or intermediary puts IP rights to a single technology or a portfolio of technologies on the auction block. Within the conditions and methods set for the auction, potential buyers review the IP and bid for it. The highest bid wins the IP rights. IP auctions can enable an SME to limit transaction costs when performing open innovation. IP auctions are typically used in two circumstances: (1) as a way to dispose of IP with less market traction or which are unnecessary for the current owner and (2) as a way to maximize revenues for very valuable IP, as a bidding war can optimize revenues to the seller or licensor.

In this chapter, we provide the basics of the IP auction model and then go on to look at what can be considered hybrid models being implemented right now and which are likely to be increasingly used in the near future. Unlike "pure" IP auctions, the hybrids introduce flexibility. For example, an example of hybrid auction is one where the winning bid does not necessarily have to be the highest one in monetary terms but it is the one with the best combination of a pecuniary offer together with a business or industrial plan to develop the IP and bring it to market. Therefore, this chapter also provides some useful tools for knowing whether or not to participate in, or use yourself, an IP auction and what forms and approaches make the most sense from the perspective of both the IP holder and IP bidder.

Definitions

Omnis definitio periculosa in Latin means that every definition can be dangerous as it can be easily misinterpreted or outdated. This holds true especially if the term has a general definition beside a specific one. For example, the term SME. By now, we all know that *SME* stands for *small and medium-sized enterprise*, which is a phrase with a certain meaning by default in English. It refers to a business with certain dimensions. The point is that an SME has a different legal definition according to the jurisdiction where the enterprise is located. In the European Union, the conditions (in terms of employees and revenues) that a company has to meet to be defined an SME are different from those provided in Japan.

Another example relates to brokerage activities. In general, as briefly mentioned in the introduction to this chapter, the *broker* is an agent who acts as intermediary upon consideration to facilitate certain transactions. For the purpose of this chapter, though, a broker has to be considered any entity in the business of buying or acquiring the right to sell IP rights to others. The broker acts as intermediary between those who own a technology and the technology seekers. It is not necessary that the broker be paid to provide the service or information relevant for making buy and sell decisions by either the original owner of the rights or the seeker interested or potentially interested in buying the rights.

IP auction is the last concept that we interpret in a more flexible way in this chapter. Usually an auction is a bidding process where the highest bidder wins. As previously noted, we discuss hybrid models in which it is not necessary for the bidder offering the most money to win. We also present a model where the rights transferred at the end of the auction are not the entire set of proprietary rights protecting the technology but rather the licensing rights.

The takeaway is that the best way to approach the world of tech transfer and IP monetization is to be extremely flexible in interpreting potential solutions and to be always aware of the legal feasibility and restrictions that different business models might have in a specific jurisdiction.

IP Brokerage: From "Push" to "Pull"?

Usually IP brokerage involves private firms that provide paid services to firms and individuals. However, with universities, research hospitals, government labs, foundations, and others developing technology, brokerage may involve providing services to a not-for-profit organization, which, by definition, is not functioning to make profits but rather for the social benefit that can be achieved through its activities. In this section, we focus on the latter.

The nature of these activities is often summarized as a "pushing" exercise in which ideas and technologies are presented to potential licensees or buyers with the hope that they will generate some interest. What makes this effort more difficult in today's global technology marketplace is the outstanding number of available technologies. There are way more inventions and technologies than there are companies interested in making and marketing them. In fact, the number of technologies actually licensed from universities and research centers constitutes just a small fraction of the portfolios of these entities. The vast majority of the available technologies end up in the file drawers of the institution, generating no real social or monetary benefit beyond the dissemination of knowledge through publications and presentations at meetings.[2]

Why does this happen? Usually, universities and research centers have offices called tech transfer offices, knowledge transfer offices, technology-licensing organizations, or some other term depending on the country and whether they are for a governmental or nonprofit research entity. We shall use the term *technology transfer offices* (*TTOs*) to refer to these offices.

TTOs receive notices of inventions conceived internally (called *invention disclosures*). Then the staff of the office evaluates the inventions, and decides whether or not to file for a patent application. What comes next

---

[2] This is unless the said university or research center is in a jurisdiction in which the size of the portfolio of a public organization might be linked to incentives provided by the central government. For example, in some jurisdictions, the simple act of filing a certain number of patent applications might give the right to the filing entity to claim monetary bonuses to be added to the general funding sources.

is really unpredictable. The technologies now have a patent application or a granted patent associated with them, so they can be protected (assuming the patent applied for issues). They need to be licensed out or assigned to someone who could actually use them and, even better, make profits that generate royalties for the institution. For that, however, it is not sufficient for the technologies to be promising; somehow, links to the industrial world need to exist or be built in order for transactions to occur.

It is a matter of fact that the United States is the by far the most profitable country on the planet in terms of technology transfer activities performed by universities and research centers, but even in this country, most of these TTOs lose money when their costs of operation are subtracted from the revenues generated by licensing. For this reason, technology transfer is ultimately an activity, which has to be at least partially justified by its social value (the so-called third mission of universities after education and research). If only the monetary return on investment was considered, technology transfer would have a hard time justifying its existence to senior management and boards of trustees.

The end result is that most universities in the world license out or assign just a small fraction of their IP. Further, most of the technologies in these institutions are, at best, at a benchtop proof-of-concept level of maturity, which means the ones that do get licensed are seldom big money makers. The consequence is these offices are pretty far from reaching the break-even point at the end of the fiscal year.

For SMEs, this is a great opportunity. Knowing that there is an abundance of technologies that are waiting to be licensed and further developed, SMEs can switch from a push model, in which they rely on brokers or tech transfer office staff are paid to facilitate transactions, to a pull model in which they go directly to the source, to the institutions owning the technology. The SME rather than the broker can be the one "buying low" so they may later "sell high." By monitoring the research literature relevant for their product lines and visiting relevant departments at nearby institutions, it is possible to identify interesting technologies. They can also contact the TTOs of leading universities and other research organization in the fields of interest. TTOs usually welcome enquiries, as their job is to license the technology and, as we just saw, it is not easily done. The Association of University Technology Managers

(AUTM) (www.autm.net), the largest global society of technology transfer professionals runs a portal called the Global Technology Portal where its members post their offerings. It is at www.gtp.autm.net/. Other ways to find technology are presented in the following sections.

Be aware not everything an institution has may be publically offered. Disclosure usually takes place after some form of IP protection has been filed for. There also might be cases in which a technology, even if developed by a university or research center, cannot be publicized and be available to be licensed due to the funding source, legal system, existence of codevelopment agreements, and so on.

The following sections will describe unconventional brokers, that is, online intermediaries that operate at no cost for the user that can further the possibilities to switch from the push to the pull model, especially as far as SMEs are concerned.

Easy Access IP

One of the first examples of initiatives offering an opportunity to SMEs for accessing available technologies coming from universities and research centers is Easy Access IP (EAIP), which is an international consortium of universities and research institutions around the world.[3] The project is based on the assumption that university-developed technologies are pretty often at an early stage of development and do require additional investment and product development efforts to reach the market. EAIP, through its licensing schemes, allows companies and individuals free non-exclusive licenses to these technologies by following a simple procedure. Although there are no up-front fees, running royalties, or other payments, easy access licenses do require the licensee to acknowledge the originator's (i.e., university or research center) contribution and to report their progress in the development and commercialization.

---

[3] Members of the Easy Access IP initiative are located in several countries. Among its members, it is worth mentioning the presence of the European Organization for Nuclear Research (CERN), the King's College London, the University of Glasgow, the University of Copenhagen, the University of Technology Sydney, and the University of Ottawa.

The EAIP license is granted after a valuation of the business plan submitted by the applicant, and if there are several applicants, there might be a competitive process in which the most promising plan will prevail. Therefore, the EAIP scheme is a great opportunity to explore for SMEs that are eager to start a project around a novel technology, have the means to develop it, and the interest to create a potentially long-lasting relationship with the originator of the technology. The almost absence of a negotiation phase (since the contracts are extremely lean) and the royalty-free licensing model can definitely be important incentives.

The specific license agreement used may vary from institution to institution. Nonetheless, all the members share four basic principles, which shape their agreements:

- Universities and research centers exist to create and disseminate knowledge. The wider the dissemination, the greater the benefit.
- Universities and research centers should encourage the creation of positive societal impacts from their research.
- Simple agreements and procedures allow the parties involved in a transaction to do deals quicker and easier.
- Agreements between the parties formed through an easy access license should be the beginning of a long-lasting relationship.

The members of EAIP do not deal with all of their inventions using the easy access license. Inventions that are likely to be big hits or are at higher stages of maturity and thus more likely to be licensed and generate profits are marketed and licensed using traditional approaches. But for SMEs with research and development (R&D) capability, the EAIP approach can provide an excellent value proposition.

Those interested in knowing more about the process introduced by EAIP or in the technologies available should visit the EAIP website at http://easyaccessip.com or view the individual members' dedicated pages, like the one managed by the CERN (Figure 2.1).

An additional source of information to have access to the technology listing of the consortium is the community section on the iBridge

Knowledge Transfer

CERN Easy Access IP

CERN Easy Access IP is a new opportunity to benefit of CERN's Intellectual Property.

The scheme involves making some of CERN's technologies available free of royalties, released only to partners who can best develop them to benefit the economy and society.
If you would like to know more about CERN Easy Access IP or other technology transfer opportunities, please contact CERN's Technology Transfer Office.

The following technologies are available under the CERN Easy Access IP scheme:

3D Magnetic sensor calibrator

This is an innovative device for calibrating magnetic field with high resolution. The technology measures all three axes of the magnetic field, by performing a scan over the full unit sphere, independent of its orientation relative to the magnetic field.

[read more]

Figure 2.1 Easy IP Access page and available technologies

Source: The CERN website.

Network (see the next section for a detailed description) website.[4] The site (Figure 2.2) allows a user to peruse all of the available technologies, get acquainted with potential advantages and uses of the inventions and technologies, and get in touch with the case manager directly, thanks to an internal messaging system.

iBridge Network

Another source of available technologies (briefly mentioned in the previous section) that can be consulted at no cost is the platform (Figure 2.3) called iBridge Network, which is managed by the Innovation Accelerator Foundation Inc., located in the United States. Among other purposes, the Foundation operates the iBridge to promote the transfer of technology,

---

[4] For more information about the available technologies on the iBridge site, please visit the community section, available at www.ibridgenetwork.org/#!/profiles/9070694345907?new.

Figure 2.2 Account of University of New South Wales Australia

Source: iBridge Network website.

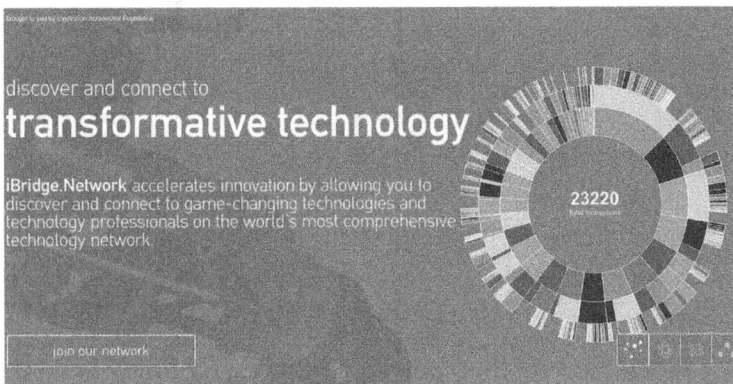

Figure 2.3 Infographics of the iBridge Network

Source: iBridge Network website.

sharing of research, and formation of collaborative efforts to advance scientific knowledge.

As of August 2015, the portal featured more than 23,000 available innovations. The sources of the technologies vary (although the majority come from the United States). The user interface allows you to create personal accounts in which your technology needs be presented to encourage future matches. Every profile shows a description of the technology in question with advantages, potential applications, and an internal messaging system that allows those interested to contact directly the technology manager for further information. Like the AUTM Global Technology Portal, the iBridge Network constitutes another valuable tool for SMEs by enabling them to examine thousands of available technologies at a single web portal simply by creating a free online account.

Enterprise Europe Network

The closest counterpart to the iBridge Network in Europe is probably the online database of the Enterprise Europe Network (EEN). The EEN, comprising over 600 partners in 52 countries, is Europe's largest network of contact points providing information and support for SMEs interested in innovation, knowledge and technology transfer practices, and other cooperation initiatives in the European Union's (EU's) programs. Among the many SME-focused services, examples are targeted market intelligence and personalized support.

The EEN also contains Europe's largest database of business and technology opportunities as the EU hopes to facilitate effective relationships between partners located in many countries and working across the innovation spectrum. As of August 2015, the EEN database claimed to contain more than 23,000 profiles, which, interestingly enough, is around the number of innovations present on the iBridge site (see Figure 2.3). There are hundreds of contact points in all of the EU countries as well as in other high-tech-oriented countries such as Israel, Japan, the United States, Korea, and the like (52 countries in all). The immediate value for technology-scouting activity by SMEs is its database of partnership opportunities. In the following (Figure 2.4) there is a screenshot showing the search panel of the database with its filtering features.

A search performed on August 30, 2015, gave the following results (Figure 2.5). On that day, the database contained 256 technology offers uploaded in the last month. The interesting fact about this result is that the database does not only contain available technologies that are protected by patents. In fact, in many instances, the offer concerns the joint development of a (patented or patent-pending) technology with a partner or the transfer of a trade secret to or its utilization with a potential partner.

The database is updated with new profiles on a weekly basis, and the requests for more information are channeled to the relevant contact

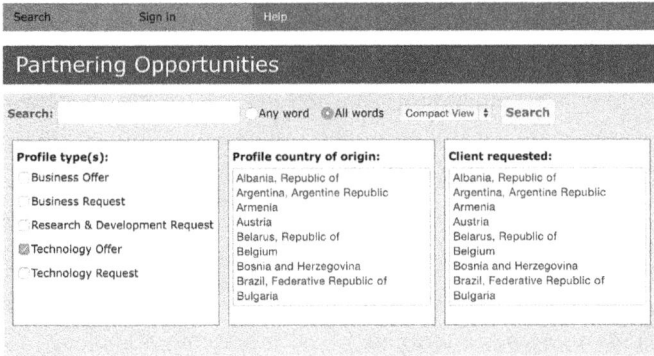

Figure 2.4 EEN database—search panel

Source: EEN database.

Title of Profile	Country	Type	Date
Algae harvesting technology	Germany	Tech. Offer	2015-08-27
Long Read-Range UHF-RFID Tags for Optical Discs	Spain	Tech. Offer	2015-08-10
UHF-RFID Near-field Antenna for Retail Applications	Spain	Tech. Offer	2015-08-08
Simple & quick solution "out-of-the-box" to time competition. Already approved and tested.	Spain	Tech. Offer	2015-08-26
Efficient data processing, software engineering and lossless data compression systems for Big Data scenarios.	Spain	Tech. Offer	2015-08-08
Proven open-source platform and technical support for Smart City solutions	Spain	Tech. Offer	2015-08-10
Method of quartz crystal microbalance with dissipation measurements (QCM-D), its application in research and the...	Ukraine	Tech. Offer	2015-08-25

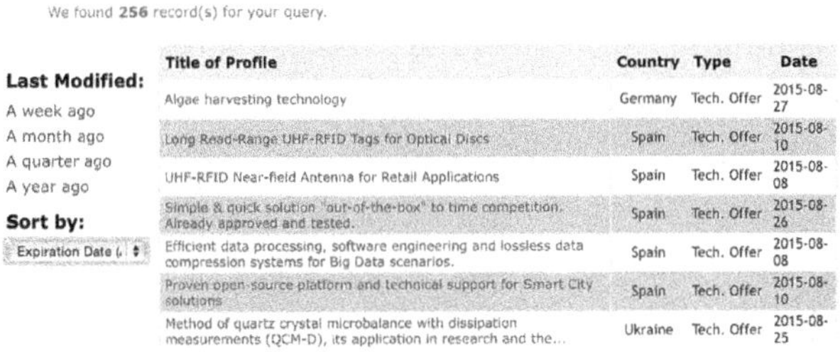

Figure 2.5 EEN database—Technology offers

Source: EEN Database, August 30, 2015.

point, who is then able to provide additional information to those making inquiries about the technology available.

The Japan Technology Transfer Helpdesk

In July 2015, the EU-Japan Centre for industrial Cooperation[5] in Japan launched its technology transfer helpdesk, called the Japan Technology

[5] Established in 1987, the EU-Japan Centre for Industrial Cooperation is a unique venture between the European Commission and the Japanese government. It is a nonprofit organization aimed at promoting all forms of industrial, trade, and investment cooperation between the EU and Japan and at improving EU and Japanese companies' competitiveness and cooperation by facilitating exchanges of experience and know-how between EU and Japanese businesses.

Transfer Helpdesk. The portal, probably publicly available from the beginning of 2016, will provide information about available technologies from Japanese universities and research centers. Its objective is to facilitate international licensing, especially toward Europe. The portal provides additional resources that help non-Japanese SMEs understand the procedures for the granting of IP rights in Japan. These resources will include informational videos and other media. As with the other platforms, relevant contacts are found with the technologies so that the initial interaction between the technology seeker and the technology provider can be as easy and direct as possible. Professionals offering IP transaction services will be listed too in order to create a virtual "one-stop shop" for those seeking technologies stemming from Japanese universities and research entities. The portal will, at a later stage, showcase technologies originating from EU universities and research centers as well.

We emphasize these are only examples. The World Intellectual Property Organization and many others also have portals. Indeed, just as there is a surplus of technology available for acquisition in the world, it appears we are entering a period where there is also a surplus of free websites facilitating access to them. SMEs, which are widely viewed as the engines of the next phase of global economic development, are in the enviable position of being the primary targets for these sites supported by associations, governments, foundations, and nongovernmental organizations.

IP Auctions: How Do They Work?

IP auctions, in principle, work like any other sort of auction. There are bidders and sellers (which includes licensors) and an auctioneer, who may also be the seller. At the end of the auction, the IP owner parts with the IP rights in exchange for an amount of money (or money and other "good things") bid.

The EU-Japan Centre for Industrial Cooperation has become an effective bridge between European and Japanese business people and developed a valuable policy analysis capacity on industrial and other public policies having an impact on business in the EU and Japan.

Usually, the individuals or companies selling or licensing through IP auctions want nothing more than to make as much money as they can. Universities, research hospitals, government labs, or other research centers all can participate in auctions unless some specific law or regulation in their country prevents participation in those kinds of activities.

An SME participating in an auction should be aware that the sellers are normally looking to exit the technology profitably. Acquiring the IP rights to technology is not a problem. However, if the SME is looking to license a technology inexpensively in a way that includes a collaboration with, and access to the know-how of, the inventor, it may be better to work through the public (or private) intermediaries mentioned earlier in this chapter or directly go to a university or research center. Approach their TTO and explore the available portfolio. Where you see interesting technology, ask them to put you in touch with the inventor so you can gauge the interest in a potential joint development effort.

IP auctions took off in the United States in the early 2000s and spread globally. Originally, like the auctions of cattle and art you see in the movies, they were physical events in which people actually went to the auction venue to meet the owners of the IP or their representatives and "kick the tires." After that, the auction took place. Nowadays, there are several online providers that offer virtual auctions, often on an asynchronous schedule over a period of days or weeks. Such auctioneers charge lower fees since the cost of the physical auction is replaced by the "simple" management of a website.

IP Auctions and Hybrid Models: The Best Recipe for an SME?

There are some hybrid models of IP auctions that are better for SMEs, which typically do not have as much cash as bigger firms. In any auction, the anticipated benefit to the IP is that they will make more profit out of the transaction than if they did a private negotiation with only one party, as those involved in the auction will raise the bids about what they might otherwise offer, in order to win. After all, buyers have some figure in mind for the real value of the IP. They are trying to buy it as far below as possible. The threat of others winning drives them up toward their cap.

Where the price paid by the winner is not just an up-front cash payment but also running royalties, or where the seller is interested in seeing their technology used and generating social benefits in addition to making money, a different dynamic comes into play. Now it is important that the technology actually make it to market. So the up-front price paid alone should not determine the winner. The biggest up-front payment may not generate the most net discounted cash flow or the best combination of cash and social benefit.

The bidder willing to pay the most money may not be the most likely to actually bring the technology into use. We can easily imagine a scenario where a large firm bids high to win, so a potentially superior technology to theirs never makes it to market. That the winner will develop and market cannot be taken for granted in situations where the only criterion is who pays the most at the time of the auction. An additional criterion may be that you have to take it to market. That kind of auction favors SMEs that are nimble and have a good track record at commercialization.

Auctions provide SMEs with flexibility when acquiring and exiting technologies. A start-up selling a technology through a hybrid auction with the two criteria of price and commercialization success may find the winning bid placed by another start-up. In an auction of a portfolio, a single SME may even play the role of an IP owner or seller and a bidder or licensee at the same time. The wonderful thing about auctions is this: When it is your auction, you make the rules.

We anticipate a flurry of creativity in IP auction models over the next decade as they become increasingly virtual and global. Some of the elements present in other IP marketplaces, like the one managed by the EAIP consortium, will probably show up in the structure of IP auctions involving public entities like universities (recall that the EAIP model requires the potential licensee, in order to persuade the originator of the technology to grant a license, to submit an application with a business plan that clarifies what economic and social benefits will result from the license and how they will be obtained). Where business plans are required, the rules of the auction can allow for reclaiming the IP rights when the plan is not followed or fails, as that would be a breach of contract. In the traditional auction format, that is not possible because there are no rights to the technology retained by the seller.[6]

Since IP rights can be parceled out in a variety of ways (field of use, activity permitted, exclusivity, time, geography, etc.), there is no reason the auction cannot sell only part of the IP rights, thereby creating a legal basis for reclaiming the technology where anticipated results are not pursued or obtained. Literally, anything permitted in a traditional licensee–licensor agreement can be made part of the rules for the auction. This way, the owner of the technology would still be the owner even after a successful auction and would indeed have the right to exercise some control over the management of the technology and be able to contractually impose on the licensee obligations to implement the business plan submitted at the time of the auction. A breach of the licensing agreement entered into at the time of the auction would always allow the technology owner to terminate the license and would make him free to dispose of the IP rights in question at his will.

Conclusions

It is a great time to be a small company. It is not infrequent to see companies with fewer than 100 employees and disruptive business models transform industrial sectors.

For SMEs using technology, it is truly a great time because there are so many available technologies out there, it is pretty much a buyer's market. The trick is to know how to find it and acquire it. With the Internet, finding it is a lot easier. Today, a company from Italy with three employees is able to license a technology from an American university and a Japanese research center just by looking at the available portfolios online. Because IP transactions are so frequent, the legal format for agreements is now relatively form driven. Most universities, research hospitals, government labs, and nonprofit R&D institutes post their license agreements online.

---

[6] Unless the laws of a legal system would regulate the auction in which purchases might be terminated if a specific condition (not related to the payment) occurs.

If the agreement is acceptable, all there is to negotiate are the economic terms. There is no need to fly over to another continent to meet executives and lawyers and have endless meetings. Companies interested in selling or licensing their technology can do the same thing.

IP auctions also make acquiring or selling technology straightforward. Auction houses are online and new forms of auction structures are being adopted to meet the needs of the parties in specific economic sectors. IP is no longer esoteric.

The result is that the spectrum of opportunities for an SME has increased exponentially. A simple query in a search engine can give an exact idea of the portals where available technologies are described at no cost other than the labor to do the search. The subsequent steps are straightforward, as has been mentioned repeatedly in this chapter. Therefore, there is no obstacle now for a small company to seek, find, and eventually license or purchase a technology from a university, individual, or other company even if it is on the other side of the planet.

CHAPTER 3

Technology Transfer

Phyllis Speser, JD, PhD, RTTP

How You Make Money—the Framework

Today, technology is almost a commodity. There is a lot of it around. If a small and medium enterprise (SME) is looking to in-license or buy, it often is a "buyers' market." It is a good time to be cherry picking or just building a portfolio to scare off and fend off competitors.

Most of the technological inventions out there will never make it to market. There are all sorts of reasons why. The most common reasons are:

(1) The inventions are immature, which means they suffer from high technical risk (will they work?); and

(2) The market is uncertain (will products and services based on them sell?). This technical and market risk increases the discounting in a net discounted cash flow analysis, making it appear financially risky to invest in licensing the technology.
Exacerbating matters is

(3) Intellectual property (IP) risk (can it be patented, was it already invented and disclosed, is it not protected in critical countries, etc.?); and

(4) Firm-specific risk (does the inventing organization know how to commercialize it or does the potential licensee know how to absorb it, adapt it for the market, and sell and support it?).

Ironically, all these risks create a business opportunity for SMEs, if they have the technical skills to mature the technology themselves (internally or by contracting) and to bring it to market and support it, once there. The reason for the business opportunity is that governments around the world have pots of money (gap funding) for maturing technology for which only small firms can compete. If an SME can either (1) gain access to the technology under a no-cost research license with an option to license to make, use, and sell, or (2) obtain a low-cost license to make, use, and sell, that SME can compete for government funding to mature the technology. Maturing the technology increases the value of the technology. The result is a classic buy low, sell high. The irony, of course, is the more risky the investment, the lower the price of acquisition. Yet if the small company can be paid to mature the technology, it has very little risk from the activity of spinning up the technology. Instead, if the SME is paid to mature the technology by the government, it may even make a profit. At worse, assuming there is a market for the technology, it is laying part of the costs of product development off on the government.

Because out-licensing these inventions is often a problem for research institutions like universities, research hospitals, government labs, and nonprofit institutes, most research institutions now have special offices called technology transfer offices (TTOs). These offices have the authority to sell and license technology for the institution. Usually, they also do cooperative research and development (R&D) agreements. As part of their job, they collect, document, and evaluate inventions. They determine which ones should be protected via patent or copyright and frequently manage that process. They also do the deals, as already noted. These offices can help you find what you are looking for. Just remember they are also the ones who will negotiate with you the terms of any deal.

Figure 3.1 depicts how technology transfer looks from the perspective of a TTO. Note there are two primary ways institutions make money off technology transfer: licensing or obtaining sponsored research funding in exchange for an option to license the resulting technology. Everything else is a variant of one of these two themes. For example, if professors or postdocs form a new company (a spinout), the TTO still licenses institution-owned technology to that new company. If the institution sets up a cooperative research center, then the companies involved pay a membership fee in exchange for option right to exclusively or nonexclusively license technology developed.

Here is how it plays out on the SME's books. When the SME acquires the technology, there is a series of expenses. These include licensing up-front fees (if any) plus any milestone payments, the cost of finding

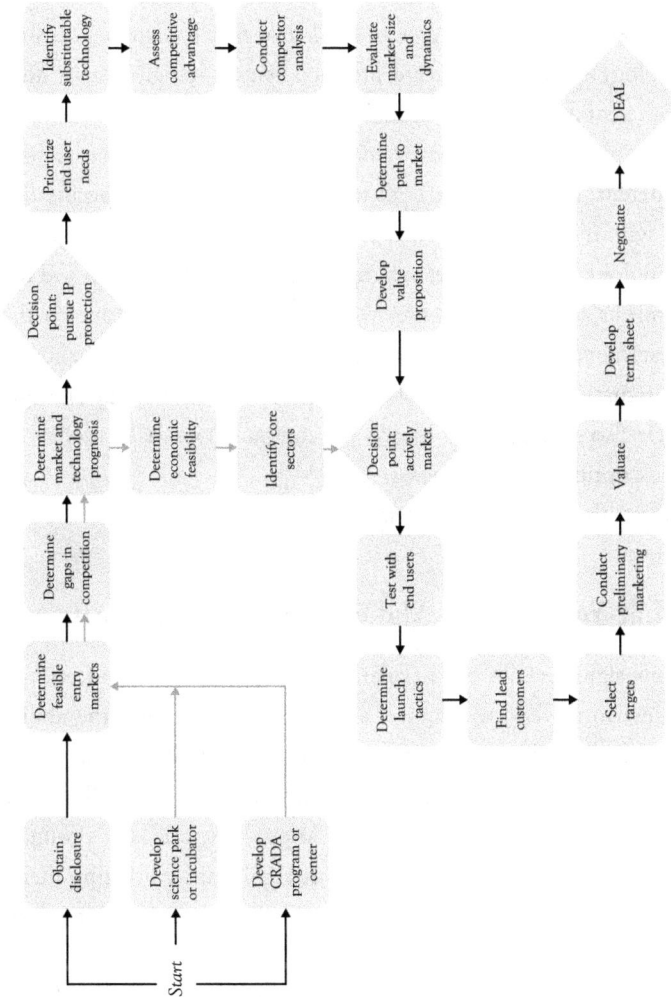

Figure 3.1 Technology transfer from the perspective of a TTO

Abbreviations: CRADA, cooperative research and development agreement.

the technology and doing due diligence on it, and the cost of negotiating and closing the deal. These expenses show up on the income statement as expenses. Depending on how the chart of accounts is structured, these expenses may be part of the cost of goods sold or in the overhead or general and administrative accounts. At this time, there is most likely no revenue, but the SME's intangible asset value increases on the balance sheet regardless of whether the technology goes to market or not. It increases because any technology relevant for future products is an intangible asset and, assuming the company is good enough to win government R&D awards, goodwill is higher. Government awards are a sign the company is technically competent, which reduces both technical risk and firm-specific risk associated with the SME's IP. Hence, two bumps in intangible asset value. If the technology actually makes it to market, revenues will go up and the revenues minus associated expenses will increase the gross profit on the income statement. Furthermore, if the technology is significant enough to cause fluctuations in the value of the company's stock, the option value of the stock also goes up. That means the company can make money by selling stock options if it so chooses.

Of course, the devil is in the detail.

What You Need to Make Money—the Details

To make any significant money at open innovation, you need four things: technologies worthwhile to acquire, a way to acquire them, the ability to bring them to market, and customers who will buy them. Please note whenever we use the term "technology" or "technologies," we will include as part of the technology the invention, know-how, and any products or services or processes based upon them or significantly utilizing them. We include both in-licensing and buying all the rights to a technology (also called assignment).

The method we use to figure out these four things is called backward chaining. You start with the desired end state, and then you determine what is needed to have it. Then, having thought backward, you plan forward—starting from where you are today. You move from there to where you need to be. In open innovation, backward chaining leads us from customers to technologies to acquire, to negotiating to acquire them. The ability to bring them to market is addressed as part of determining what to acquire.

Backward Chaining With Customers

People want new technologies for all sorts of reasons. But for open innovation, the best reason is a pressing need that cannot currently be adequately met. This need drives the features and functionality customers will desire in a product or service and the price they will pay to get it. Businesses that talk to their customers and listen to them usually have some ideas of where market opportunities lie.

Let us illustrate this with an example; suppose you are a farmer with a lot of acreage under cultivation. Let us also suppose you are in California's Central Valley—one of the great food-growing regions of America. Ideally, you only want to give your plants water when they need it. The same is true for other inputs (e.g., fertilizer). In both cases, eliminating the unnecessary application of inputs reduces expenses and, assuming solid revenues, increases profit. In the case of California, four years of drought has created a situation where limiting the amount of water may make the difference between staying in business or bankruptcy, because water is scarce and wells are running dry. The problem is that limiting inputs to only what is necessary for crop health requires good data about soil moisture, plant respiration, disease, and so on.

On a large farm of thousands or millions of acres, collecting that data can be time-consuming and expensive. The U.S. government has recently issued rules governing the use of unmanned aerial vehicles (UAVs) in civilian airspace. For large acreage farms, using UAVs to collect data is now a viable option. As more data becomes available, new approaches to data analysis also become viable.

At the major trade shows, like Commodity Classic, which focuses on corn, soy, wheat, and sorghum, there were lots of interest in both UAVs and space-based data to support precision agriculture. Not surprisingly, the major vendors of crop management software are now highlighting how they can incorporate aerial data. These product enhancements result from vendors talking with, and listening to, their customers. Smaller firms were introducing UAVs and data or image analysis packages that either are stand-alone products or designed to work with one of the major vendor packages. It is an area ripe for open innovation as there is a lot of defense and earth observation software that could be (and already is being) repurposed for use in precision agriculture. (Which is why the National Aeronautics and Space Administration's [NASA's] Goddard Space Flight Center's TTO has an initiative focused on precision agriculture. Goddard is the world's largest earth observation center.)

Listening to customers and talking with stakeholders and experts is a good way to find out what customers in your market might buy. Your market can be one your SME already services. It can also be one you are interested in penetrating. In either case, the first step is to identify and understand needs.

Needs always can be quantified on scales.

Ordinal scales are constructed on the basis one is more than two, two is more than three, and three is more than four. We do not know if the interval between one and two is the same as the one from two to three or three to four. We also do not know if zero makes any sense as a measurement on this scale. We just know it is about more and less. An example is love. You tell your spouse, I love you more than words can tell. Desirability of a product is measured by an ordinal scale.

Other scales can also be used. Interval scales have equal intervals, but zero is arbitrary. An example is years. The year zero on a calendar does not mean there were no years before that.

Ratio scales have meaningful zeros. Absolute zero is where there is no heat energy left in a substance. Zero celsius is where water freezes. Distance is a ratio scale as is power consumption.

What we want to know is needs on three dimensions: performance, ease of use, and price.

Performance consists of the hard, measurable engineering specifications. Usually it is measured on ratio scales or interval scales. It uses this much power. It is this big. It blocks this much radiation. Whatever. A good way to think about performance is to think about the patent claims you would make for a technology. Efficacy in attaining those claims is the performance. An inhalable flu vaccine works if it gives the user some percentage of certainty that a person will not have the flu for some period of time.

Ease of use consists of factors that make a technology easier or harder to adopt. Usually it is measured on interval or ordinal scales. If a technology requires extensive training to know how to use it, special infrastructure, and so on, then the hassle of adopting and implementing it rises. Obviously, ease of use is context sensitive. A computer easy for you to use may not be so for your 93-year-old grandmother.

Price is what something costs. It is measured in currency, which is a ratio scale. There cannot be "sticker shock" or no one will buy the technology. What if sticker shock varies from application (field of use) to application. In each arena, buyers are used to spending some level of money. A quick way to estimate how much is to look at multiples of 10. One dollar, 10 dollars, 1,000 dollars, 10,000 dollars, and so on. When I buy a new car, a price in the $20,000-to-$30,000 range is reasonable. When I buy a used car, however, a price in the $5,000-to-$10,000 range seems reasonable unless the car is only a year or two old and has low mileage.

The final reason is UMPF. UMPF is a made-up term, which means there is some imperative to buy this good now rather than later. UMPF is measured on an ordinal scale. When water is scarce, home gardeners are more likely to buy drip irrigation systems. When it is plentiful, they are less likely to.

The point is, if we collect data about needs, we are also collecting data on what a technology must do to be attractive to buyers. We can then assess the attractiveness of technologies for acquisition in terms of how well they fit the needs of customers in markets of interest (see Figure 3.2). Ideally, these needs will endure over time long enough for the SME to run through the process of acquiring it, bringing it to market, and making money off it.

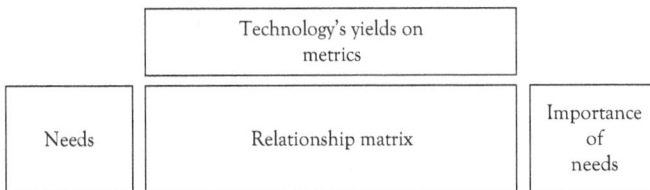

Figure 3.2 Assessing attractiveness of technologies based on buyer needs

Source: © Foresight Science & Technology 2015.

Finding Technology to Acquire

Usually, a technology is not a perfect fit with a set of needs. So when doing due diligence on a technology, we want to know more than what it does today on relevant metrics and what it is anticipated to be able to do when R&D is completed. We also need to understand the flex (flexibility) of the technology to be adapted better to the needs of potential customers. Typically, changing yield on one metric will adversely affect yield on another one. The trick is to be able to degrade trade-off yields on low-priority metrics to improve yields on high-priority ones (see Figure 3.3).

As the old adage goes, there is more than one way to skin a cat, and typically, there is more than one technology that can address end user needs. Just as customers have choices, so also do companies acquiring technology. By comparing yields on high-priority metrics (i.e., customer needs), an acquirer can compare the competitive advantage of various technologies. There is a large pool of empirical research that validates the commonsense view that competitive advantage is the critical factor in market success. Be aware that competitive advantage has to exist at the time the product or service will be introduced to the market. There is a dynamic system here, with both technology and customer needs having trajectories over time.

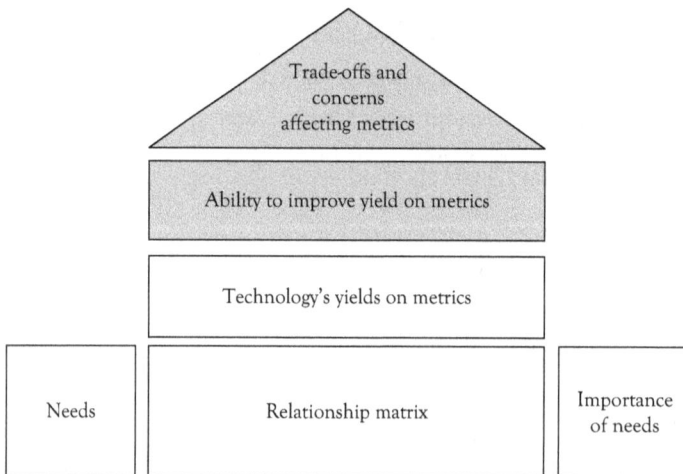

Figure 3.3 Trade-off analysis is part of technical due diligence

Source: © Foresight Science & Technology 2015.

You can use a spreadsheet to model current or potential competitive advantage and portray it graphically. Each column represents a metric. You plot the customer's desired values for the yields. Then you plot the yields of the various technologies that can address those needs either in their current state or after further development to optimize them for end user needs (see Figure 3.4).

If you want a single value to represent competitive advantage, you can normalize the values for the yields. If the significance of metrics varies significantly, you can weight them. The result is an ordinal number on a scale from 0 (the worst) to 10 (the best).

Competitive advantage mitigates market risk. Lower market risk means lower discounting and thus higher value on the balance sheet. This higher value, in turn, reflects a greater likelihood of downstream net positive cash flow from sales or licensing of the technology.

Another factor to assess when determining whether to in-license or buy a technology is IP risk. If the technology infringes the rights of others, it will be difficult to introduce. An inability to obtain strong IP protection, or any at all, may be less of an issue depending on the nature of the technology and the field of use in which it will be applied. That

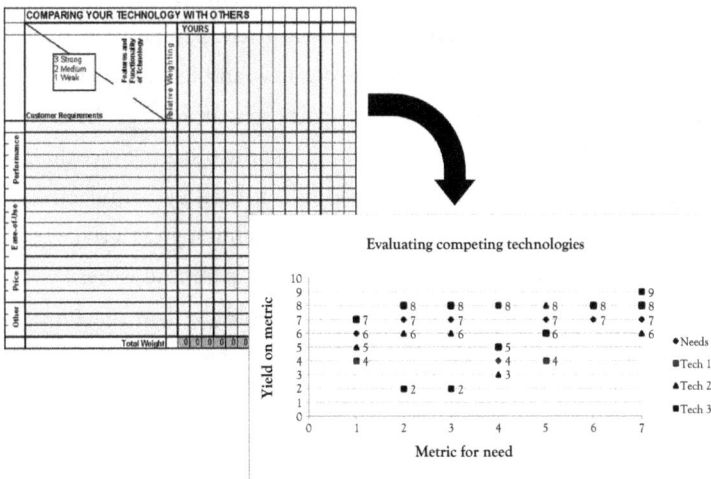

Figure 3.4 Data sheet and display for evaluating competing technologies against customer needs

Source: © Foresight Science & Technology 2015.

said, in general, obtaining an exclusive license to the IP rights can give you a monopoly position in the market or at least give you a monopoly for a specific technical approach. Good patent, copyright, mask IP, or a combination of these protects technologies from being made, sold, or used by others. Patents protect inventions; copyrights protect creative works, including software code. Masks protect the layout of the lines on chips and circuit boards.

Critical for determining the strength of IP protection is determining three things. The first is the claims made in a patent or the work submitted in a copyright or mask filing. The claims or work determines what is to be protected. The second is the priority date. In general, it is a first-to-file world. The priority date establishes who is first to file if more than one application is submitted. The third is how much time is left on a patent. If a patent has not issued, the issue becomes what is necessary to secure one. Other factors, such as whether the technology is only protected by one patent or by a group of patents (or a group of patents plus a trademark, trade secret, etc.) strengthen the IP protection. In general, IP protection in more of the jurisdictions in which customers are found is stronger than where fewer jurisdictions are covered.

Process technologies can be protected through trade secrets if they are easily copied to make products, but the products cannot be reverse engineered to determine if infringement occurred. Several years back, we worked with a university that developed a new and less expensive way to make a specialty chemical. We advised against patenting it as the chemical was a commodity and patenting would disclose the process. Since there was no way to know if the process was used or not used by manufacturers of the chemical, we recommended licensing the technology as a trade secret.

In general, there are four requirements for a patent to issue.

First, the subject matter must be protectable. By law, machines and processes are almost always patentable, while laws of nature are not. Whether software, results of genetic engineering, and so on are patentable depends on whether they are seen by the legal jurisdiction as closer to machines and processes or laws of nature.

Second, it must be novel (i.e., a new *bona fide* invention). We once were hired by a Fortune 500 company to out-license surplus patents. One was for an electric outlet with a 120-volt and a 240-volt socket.

As electric cars were about to be introduced, we determined there was a market for this technology. However, we recommended abandoning the patent because we discovered a firm had been selling these dual-voltage outlets to the public for several years before the patent held by our client had been filed.

Third, the invention must be novel, which means it is not obvious to a practitioner in the field of the invention.

Fourth, it must not have been previously disclosed to the public.

These four traits are sufficient for a design patent. Design patents protect nonfunctional, purely ornamental designs. A "spork" is an eating utensil that is both a fork and a spoon. A variety of design patents cover different looks for sporks.

Plant patents protect asexually reproduced plants and sexually reproduced plant seeds. Such plants and seeds are usually the result of a scientific experiment involving genetic engineering or crossbreeding.

What people normally think of when they hear the word patent is a utility patent. These patents have, as the name indicates, an additional requirement that the invention be useful for some human endeavor. Usefulness has to be proven through an actual or constructive reduction to practice. Theoretical utility does not count. Anyone who has seen a *Star Trek* TV show or movie knows what a teleporter is. With the discovery of quantum pairs, it is theoretically possible to see how one might be constructed. It is much more than a simple matter of engineering to build one; because the teleporter is still just an idea and not reduced to practice, it cannot at present be patented.

When evaluating technologies for their current or potential IP protection, there are a number of free and fee-for-service patent and copyright servers you can use. (You also can easily find search copyrights, trade and service marks, and masks.) My favorite free ones are the U.S. Patent and Trademark Office (www.uspto.gov/patent) and the European Patent Office (www.epo.org/searching.html). The latter includes a worldwide patent search engine. The World Intellectual Property Organization (WIPO) (https://patentscope.wipo.int/search/en/search.jsf) can also be searched for applications under the Patent Cooperation Treaty (primarily patents seeking protection in more than one country) as well as patents from member countries of WIPO.

When assessing the potential patent protection for a technology, what counts are the claims. Using a spreadsheet, you can create a tool for comparing claims of other patents and patent applications with the technology you are interested in acquiring or in-licensing (see Figure 3.5). In addition to the "closeness" or similarity of each claim, it is also important to look at content of the claims in terms of how broad and seminal they are and whether they constitute major technological breakthroughs or are more like variations of a theme.

Note that if only summary values are desired, begin by examining the first claims on their own. These claims are usually the most significant, and combining the spread from the baseline here with the spread from other claims would distort the results. As the other claims clarify and extend the first claim, next weigh and average them on their own. Place greater weight on those claims related to higher-priority needs (metrics) in the eyes of your customers.

We are now in a position to determine which technologies look most interesting, all other things being equal. The most important element of "all other things" is alignment with capabilities and resources of the firms, a topic we shall address next. Where we are is presented in Figure 3.6.

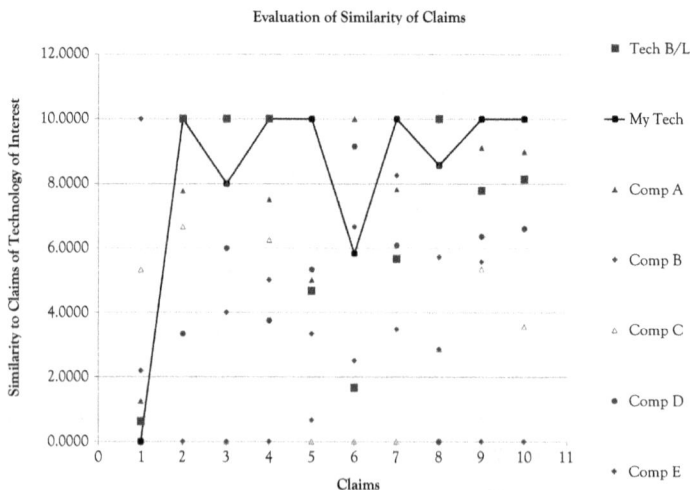

Figure 3.5 Assessing the strength of a patent

Source: © Foresight Science & Technology 2015.

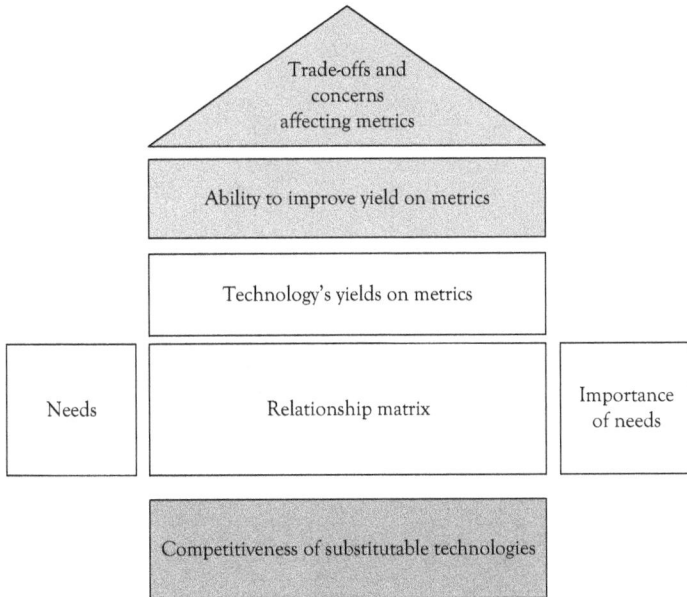

Figure 3.6 Attractiveness of technologies independent of the specific capabilities and resources of the SME

Source: © Foresight Science & Technology 2015.

The final thing to assess is firm-specific risk for the SME if it acquires the technology. Interestingly, once we have the yields customers seek on performance, ease of use, price, and UMPF, we can use those to garner insights on what we need to make and support the technology in the market. That is because the desired yields constrain the materials and parts and the production process that can be used to make the technology, and these, in turn, constrain how the technology can be transported, maintained, and repaired (see Figure 3.7).

Ideally, what you want is a strong alignment with materials, parts, and components you already use and R&D and production processes you already utilize. That makes the technology easier for you to adapt and introduce to the market.

As an example, a small firm was looking for a better way to detect cancer cells in mammography and other images. Using an open innovation approach, the firm found an image-processing technology at NASA's Goddard Space Flight Center. That technology had been originally

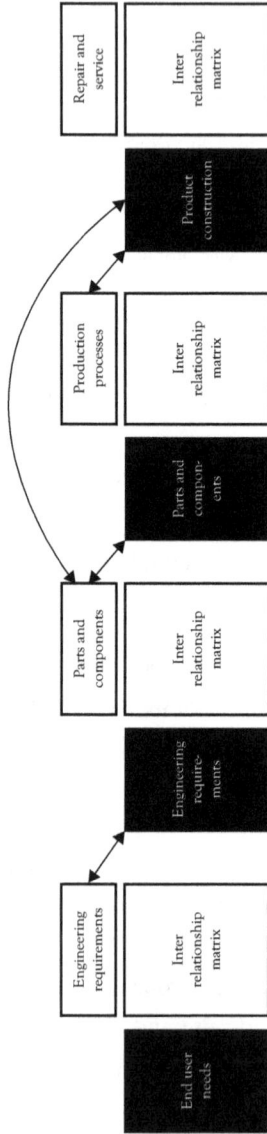

Figure 3.7 Matrix relationships between customer needs and the SME's capabilities

developed to better assess the depth of lakes from space. It was based on an invention called "Recursive Hierarchical Segmentation" (RHSEG)—a new way of combining the pixels in an image to do better recognition of features of interest. Although proven, the technology had been only used by NASA and was still too immature for commercial introduction. The small firm, Bartron Medical Imaging (www.bartron.ws/) had the absorptive capacity to recognize the value of RHSEG and to adapt it to a new use, after in-licensing it. As part of the adaption process, Bartron entered into a cooperative R&D agreement with NASA Goddard and also won a variety of government R&D awards. The product, MED-SEG, won the R&D Magazine *R&D 100 Award* for being one of the most significant new products of 2011.

Porter's value chain is another way to identify potential leverage points. Figure 3.8 in the following text, from Wikipedia (http://en.wikipedia.org/wiki/Value_chain), displays these leverage points. The primary activities depict what is needed to make, deliver, sell, and support a product or service in the market. The support activities provide the back end for

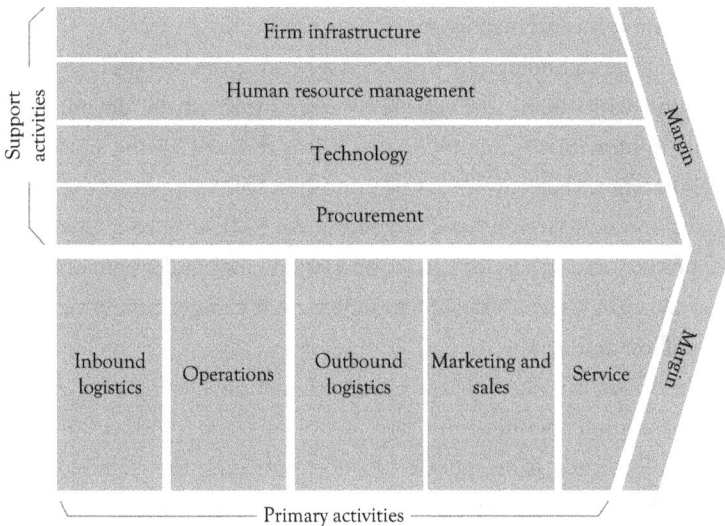

Figure 3.8 Michael Porter's value chain

Source: © Wikipedia 2015.

the primary activities. Technology includes both the acquisition of IP and maturing it for the market.

What you are seeking are technologies with strong alignment for your company, as that reduces firm-specific risk. Reducing firm-specific risk increases the value of the technology for you on the balance sheet. For example, can the same manufacturing process be used? If you can make toilet paper, you can probably make paper hand towels. If you have a strong brand name that pulls supermarket sales of toilet paper, you probably have a good shot at getting some shelf space to try selling paper towels. However, assume your only market is consumers and your only distribution channel is supermarkets; if you want to sell paper towels to institutions like airport, restaurant, school, and other commercial and industrial bathrooms, you need to become part of a different supply chain. In manufacturing, you are aligned; in distribution, you are not.

A critical metric for alignment with the company is absorptive capacity. Absorptive capacity is the ability to bring in and adapt the technology and turn it into something useful or marketable. With respect to more immature technologies, absorptive capacity requires an ability to do R&D—or at least to manage it.

Immature technologies are of interest because the best deals for SMEs are found with them. The reason is larger firms usually do not invest heavily in immature technologies unless it is through buying stock in, or collaborating with, an SME. (The second-best technologies are those with markets too small to interest a large firm. An SME may be happy with a new product that generates $1, $5, or $10 million in sales per year. Large firms are most likely seeking technologies that can generate revenues of $20 million and up.)

The House of Quality is a Quality Function Deployment tool for linking customer wishes with the capabilities and products of firms. In our adaptation, it becomes a tool for evaluating the technologies to acquire in light of customer needs and the capabilities and resources of a firm. Figure 3.9 presents this House of Quality.

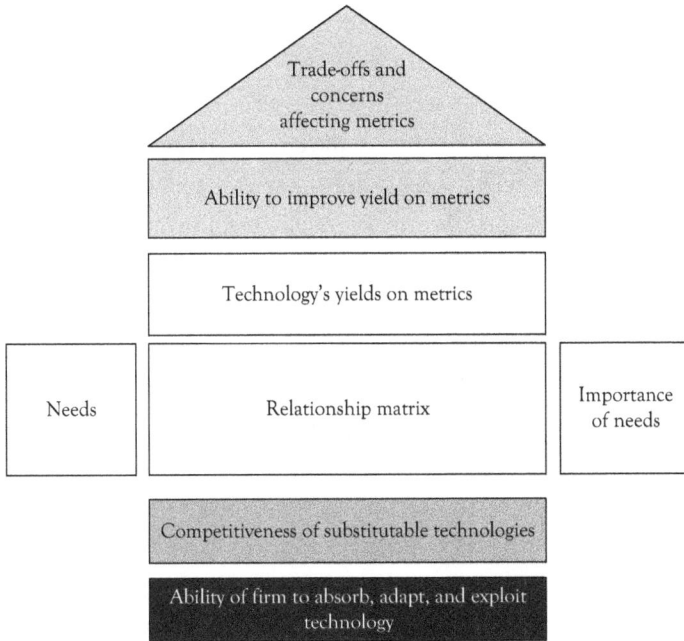

Figure 3.9 House of Quality for technology acquisition or in-licensing

Source: © Foresight Science & Technology 2015.

Planning Forward

Negotiating to Acquire Technologies

Acquiring a technology is a market transaction. In this respect, it is not different than buying a pair of shoes or a house. Technically, what is being sold is not the physical object but all or some of the rights to control the physical object. The legal transaction defines the rights (to do research with, make, use or sell or both), geographic territory (countries), field of use (markets), and exclusivity being transferred in exchange for money and other terms and conditions addressing warrantees, guarantees, liabilities, default, payment mechanisms, auditing rights, conduct and oversight of IP enforcement, and so on.

As in any market transactions, the seller (licensee) tries to sell high, and the buyer (licensor) tries to buy low. Negotiations involve convergence on a fair price.

During the convergence process, the buyer examines the IP and either makes or is given the first offer. The other party decides the price is fair or makes a counteroffer. The offering price is seldom accepted. One reason is the capitalist dynamic of buy low and sell high. Another reason is any transaction carries the risk that what you buy may not be what you expected. The anticipated patent may not issue because it infringes a previously unpublished patent issued on an application filed earlier but not published during the SME's due diligence.

When negotiating, consider all terms as part of the price. You can accept them and bear the costs of accepting them or reject them and thus expect a different price. For example, if you accept a limitation on liability, you always have the option to buy an insurance policy to protect yourself against the potential liability (e.g., the house burning down, the shoes being stolen, the IP being infringed). But the cost of that policy should impact the price paid.

That said, unlike banks that insure against bad loans, SMEs cannot expect to insure against failure to make money off the technology. It is critical that the rights being granted in the agreement allow the SME to exploit market opportunities while blocking competitors from competing against them with the same technology. As the caption to Figure 3.10 highlights, when practicing open innovation, SMEs should be seeking a monopoly position for their products.

There are a number of perspectives on how you can and cannot set a fair price. There is more consensus on what you should not do. As a buyer of technology, you should not consider a price based on what it cost to develop the technology to its current state. What was invested to develop it is irrelevant. Besides, many institutions will give you a number based on what was spent and forget to tell you which government agencies, foundations, and others may have subsidized the R&D to date. Indeed, with the overhead included on grants or sponsored research, the institution may have no net investment. But more important than any of this is why you are negotiating. You are interested in this technology because you want to make money. So the first consideration is how much money can you make and what will it cost you to make it.

You can make money in two ways. A new technology can cut your costs. Usually this is the criterion for process (production) technologies. The other way you make money is you get new or better products and services and sell those, hopefully making more profit than you did selling what you had in the past (see Figure 3.11).

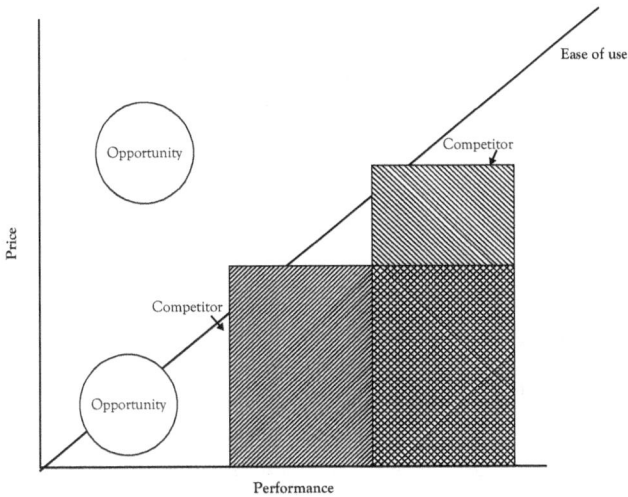

Figure 3.10 The buyer or licensee seeks a monopoly position in open innovation

Source: © Foresight Science & Technology 2015.

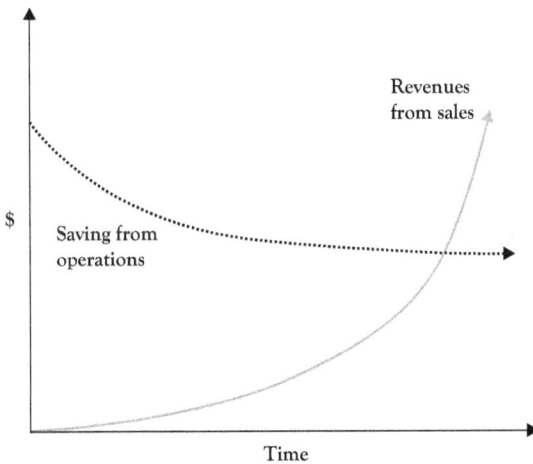

Figure 3.11 The goal of open innovation is to grow profit

Source: © Foresight Science & Technology 2015.

On the other side of the income statement are expenses, and on the balance sheet, we have liabilities. These are associated with what the technology will require to bring it to market, given its current level of maturity. Figure 3.12 presents an overview of some of the things that are needed to bring a technology to market. Among the activities are completing applied R&D (Research in Figure 3.12), obtaining any additional funding needed (Financing), designing the product or service (Design), implementing the design through engineering development and documentation (Impl and Eng), testing and evaluating (Test Mgt or Management), setting up manufacturing and controls (Manufacturing Management or Mgt and Controls or Ctrl), obtaining equipment and other processes such as quality assurance (Processes or Prc and Equipment or Equip), arranging for and conducting logistics and disposition of waste or recycling (Logistics or Log and Disposal or Disp), conducting distribution and customer service plus sales (Distribution or Dist and Service or Srvc), and of course, managing the whole process (Management, as shown in the following figure).

The mainstream view of what you should pay for a technology (or more accurately, certain rights to it) is that the price should be no more than to its contribution to the profit you can make. Otherwise you would lose money by acquiring it. Suppose the total profit from a product or service

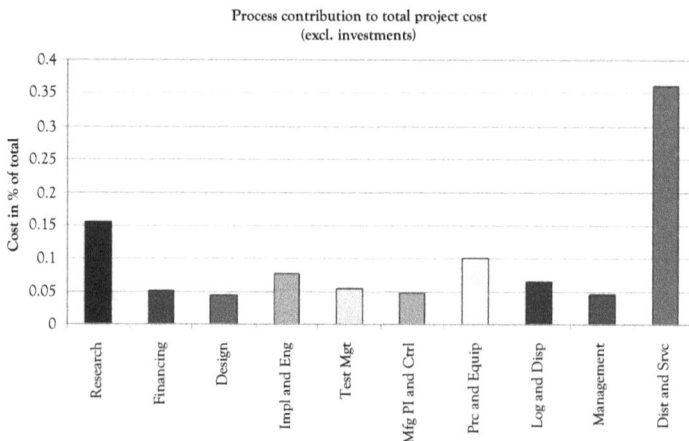

Figure 3.12 *Example of activities required to transition from R&D to the market*

Source: © Foresight Science & Technology 2015.

is $X. Suppose the product is a cell phone. We can go further and say the screen contributes around 10 percent of the profit, the keyboard another 10 percent, the central processing unit (CPU) is maybe 20 percent, the battery 10 percent, the memory 5 percent, the antenna 5 percent, the case 1 percent, the size factor 20 percent, and the apps the rest.

The percentages you use are never "correct"; they are your best guesses. Each person views the contribution to value or profit contribution of the various components differently. When we say this technology contributes Y% to the value or profit of the final product or service, what we are more accurately saying is this: In our market's population, there is a statistical tendency to view the contribution to value as Y%. In another population or at another time, that tendency might be different. (See Figure 3.9, which illustrates that the value of less weight shifts depending on the use of a computer.)

We use a different approach. What you are really buying is, of course, an intangible asset. Assets are supposed to be things you use to make money. At first glance, it seems the ceiling price (i.e., the most you should pay) should be set by how much you can make off the technology, which is equal to the technology's contribution to value or profit. But there is always a make or buy decision in product development. An SME with good absorptive capacity might do internal development of new technology with its own staff. It might also be able to buy other technology from another vendor. So what the technology is actually worth to the SME is the difference in the profit from adopting this technology versus the next best approach. (The next best approach may be zero, in which case the contribution to value method is used.)

We measure this difference by subtracting the net present value (NPV) to the company of acquiring or internally developing the second-best technology from the NPV of this technology. One part of that is the different revenues and expenses of the two technologies. The other part is time to market. This difference we call the "Present Value of the Growth Opportunity." That is what the SME is really paying for.

Figure 3.13 illustrates this concept. At the time of negotiations, the SME is formally or informally calculating the benefit of doing the deal. As the figure highlights, that benefit is either from anticipated greater NPV or it is from getting out to market (to revenues) quicker. In Figure 3.12 it is both.

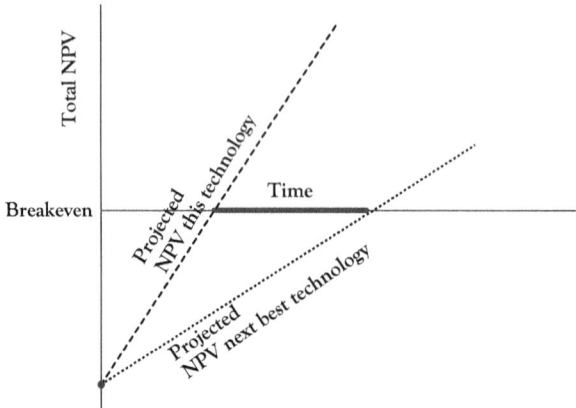

Figure 3.13 The present value of the growth opportunity is a function of net profit and time to market

Source: © Foresight Science & Technology 2015.

Ultimately, all that counts is what someone will pay and someone will accept. Prior to a deal, all value is speculative. It is fixed by the deal itself.

What is going on is called, in game theory, a "P-Beauty Contest" (where P-Beauty means Probability of Beauty). In a P-Beauty Contest, the judges are voting on who or what is the most beautiful. It can be a person or a "fair price." However, unlike a traditional beauty contest, in a P-Beauty Contest, the judges are not voting on who or what they see as most beautiful. They are voting on who or what they think everyone else will find the most beautiful. Hence the name, as the P stands for probability. The judges are voting on the probability that all the other judges will agree this specific entrant is more beautiful than the others (see http:// en.wikipedia.org/wiki/Keynesian_beauty_contest).

P-Beauty Contests are usually played over several rounds in which aggregated data depicting how everyone voted is disclosed. Over time, there is a convergence on one entrant. Interesting, when the same game is played several times, the convergence takes place quicker as people jump steps to arrive at the convergence point.

Note that repeat players in P-Beauty Contests start out with an advantage over novices if there is a statistical tendency for the games to converge in similar ways. Where that is the case, it makes sense for novices to study what has happened in similar contests in the past.

In the context of IP markets, where IP is like a commodity, the participants in a deal can look at comparable deals to see where others have converged. These prices provide a starting point for guessing what will be seen as fair in this deal. What makes other transactions comparable is that they involve similar technologies, with similar maturity and IP protection, being acquired for use in the same markets or applications. Usually it is hard to find enough comparables to use valid descriptive statistical methods, so the parties improvise by looking at ranges for all technology being acquired to use in that market or analogous technologies going into the same market.

They can also look and see what have been commonly agreed-upon terms. As we noted earlier, the way terms are defined affects the price. For example, an exclusive licensee usually has the obligation to monitor for infringement in a license. In general, the party that can best avoid or mitigate risk should be responsible for doing just that: avoiding or mitigating risk. So the licensee, who is actually making products and providing services, should bear the burden of product liability. To bear the burden means you indemnify the licensor against being sued for product liability and bear the responsibility (and the associated costs) of preventing harm due to products or services dependent upon the technology. This allocation of responsibilities and burdens makes sense because if the most qualified party handles each risk, the likelihood of the drive to market bogging down is reduced.

There is a significant transaction cost when doing a deal, so you want to keep negotiations short and on track. The idea is to use methods that encourage rapid convergence on a price. We recommend offering prices somewhere in the interquartile range as a starting point for negotiations. Unfortunately, we seldom have enough data even for that. Our fallback is to use expert panels. We survey people who have done deals in the space we are interested in. We ask them what they see as fair for a "sanitized" nonproprietary description of the technology. After listening to them, we take our best guess.

We know that a variety of other factors will affect price. In IP transactions, price has two components: fees and royalty rates. Fees are fixed payments. Royalties are paid on sales.

Typically, licensees want an up-front fee. This serves two functions. For sellers, it makes them comfortable that you actually will try to commercialize the technology. Second, it provides cash to offset out-of-pocket expenses like patenting expenses. Patenting expenses here include patent attorney fees and filing and maintenance fees. Third, if the know-how or trade secret is being transferred, and that is not considered in the royalty rate, it is paid up-front.

Unless the deal is a one-time payment, expect running royalties. These are calculated in three ways: net sales (sales – discounts + returns); gross profits (net sales – cost of goods sold); or fixed price (x dollars or x percent of price on each unit sold). If the reader has studied economics or business, he or she will recognize these should all equal the same amount—all other things being equal. But then, all other things seldom are equal and you want the one that will likely cost you the least, given how you plan to make money off the technology. Net sales is generally good for products and services that are not bulk commodities. Fixed price is generally good for bulk commodities. Gross profit is generally good for process technologies.

An NPV analysis could look at various ways of structuring a deal that all have the same NPV but different timing and amounts for fees and royalties. For example, the running royalty rate would be higher if up-front fees are lower. From the perspective of the SME, running royalties are where you want to pay for the technology, because you only pay them when you are making money. The licensor wants them up-front to lower the risk. One compromise is to move some up-front fees into milestone payments. For example, if product development and regulatory approval are completed in two years (or whatever time the parties think is reasonable), a fee of X is owed. However, if they are not, a fee of X + Y is owed every year until they are completed. **Caution:** It only makes sense to accept terms like this one if you are confident you can do what you have said you can do.

Universities, research hospitals, nonprofit and government labs, and so on will expect to recapture patenting expenses as a minimum up-front fee for an exclusive agreement. That is pretty much the norm globally. The theory behind it is the buyer is the exclusive beneficiary of the patent protection and so the buyer should pay. The counter argument is the licensor is receiving payments. That means the licensor is a beneficiary too. So at a minimum, the patenting fees should be split in accordance with some fair and reasonable principle. For example, if the payments (up-front fees and royalties) due to the licensor for its contribution to the value or profit of the product are equal to X, then the licensor should at least cover that percentage of the patenting expenses.

As noted earlier, running royalty rates are based on comparables. The best place to find them is in government databases, such as the U.S. and Canadian security and exchange commissions. In their corporate filings, companies are required to report seminal events. Often, obtaining a license is a seminal event, so the deals are reported. Sometimes the data on financial terms are redacted, or redacted for some period of years. As noted, expert panels are also a good way to come up with a "comparables" benchmark.

However the "industry average fair market value" royalty rate is determined, once you have it, it still needs to be adjusted for specifics of the technology and IP rights that are being sold here. A variety of actors come into play here. You can model them by building a simple royalty rate calculator on a spreadsheet (see Figure 3.14).

In Figure 3.14, the factors are the ones that often are raised in royalty rate negotiations. The factors in the table are illustrative, not exhaustive. The rate is the adjustment from the industry average royalty rate for this kind of technology. It moves the royalty rate up and down. The weight

Factor	Rate	Weight	Impact
Industry Norm	0.0%	0.0	0%
Significance (Breakthrough add 5-10%, Major add 0-5%%, Minor subtract 0-3%	0.0%	3.0	0%
Refinement/Maturity of Technology (High add, Low subtract)	0.0%	2.0	0%
Breadth and Strength of IP Protection (Yes add, No subtract)	0.0%	2.0	0%
Portfolio, Not Single Patent Being Licensed (Yes add, No subtract)	0.0%	2.0	0%
Exclusive Market Position in Field of Use Gained (Yes add, No subtract)	0.0%	3.0	0%
Immediate Utility in Market (Yes add, No subtract)	0.0%	2.0	0%
Commercially Successful (Already Successful in Market add, Not Yet Proven in Market subtract)	0.0%	3.0	0%
Competition Exists which Will Inhibit Ability to Exploit (Yes subtract, No add)	0.0%	1.0	0%
Foreign Rights (Yes add, No subtract)	0.0%	3.0	0%
Sales Conveyed or Highly Likely (Yes add, No subtract)	0.0%	2.0	0%
Duration (Over Ten Years add, Under Three Years subtract)	0.0%	1.0	0%
Upfront Payment Required (Yes subtract, No or Conditional add, Standard neutral)	0.0%	2.0	0%
Minimum Royalties (Yes subtract, no add, Standard neutral)	0.0%	2.0	0%
Know-How Included in Deal (Yes add, No subtract, Standard neutral)	0.0%	3.0	0%
Support/Training Provided After Initial Transfer (Yes add, No subtract, Standard neutral)	0.0%	2.0	0%
Maintenance and Enforcement Burden (Licensee subtract, Licensor add, Standard neutral)	0.0%	2.0	0%
Exposure to Liability (Yes subtract, No add, Standard neutral)	0.0%	2.0	0%
Total			0%
Add to Industry Norm			0.00%
RATE			0.000%

Figure 3.14 A royalty rate calculator

Source: © Foresight Science & Technology 2015.

can be used if some factors are much more important for the fields of use (markets) that will be granted in the license.

When we negotiate, we make a royalty rate calculator and do at least two runs. The first one is what we think is a fair price. Hopefully that is at or below what our customer is willing to pay. The second one is the initial offer or counteroffer. It is, when we represented the buyer, lower. With each factor, we include a few sentences explaining why the rate adjustment has been pegged where it is. Our experience is that the other parties respond by explaining where they disagree and why. This kind of dialogue makes negotiations smoother and quicker as you can agree their position is reasonable or point to data and logic that explains why you think they are misunderstanding the impact of the factor. In other words, we are continuing to use the model of a P-Beauty Contest and arguing over where the market would see a fair price.

Negotiations usually involve other factors that are not part of the general fair market value P-Beauty Contest. These factors are specific to the parties negotiating. With universities and equivalent research institutions, perhaps the most important one is mission. The TTO negotiators are usually juggling a balanced scorecard of several success metrics. Meeting the mission of stimulating the economy and helping SMEs may be more important than making money. If that is the case, the licensor is likely to be less aggressive on price than a corporate lab whose balanced scorecard places a lot more emphasis on making money.

There is an old adage, "First walk in the other person's shoes." Here that means if you can understand what constitutes success for the other party, you usually know pretty quickly if you can structure a win-win scenario. If you can, you share it and negotiate in good faith. If not, walk away and do not waste your time negotiating.

Obtaining "Free" Money

To spin up (i.e., mature into a product or service) a technology takes money. The best kind of money for that is other peoples' money. The best other peoples' money comes from government agencies and foundations, as it is usually "free money."

Free money is not really free. You have to write proposals, submit reports, and you may be audited to make sure you did the work you proposed. It is called "free" money because there is no equity cost. At worst, you get to lay part of your R&D costs off on the government (most likely), a foundation, or another company (least likely). At the very best, you get your R&D paid for and make a profit on it. It is a straight funding (the award) for services provided (the R&D proposed) transaction. Even better, in the United States and many other countries, the SME usually is able to retain all commercial rights in the R&D results and any data collected or created.

Free money provides revenues, goodwill, and new IP. Payments under grants and contracts are revenue. As noted earlier, the fact that you can list yourself as an award winner in a competitive program means your firm must have some technical capabilities as well as enough marketing skills to write a successful proposal. Knowledge and insights gained during the R&D, which can be exploited for commercial purposes, are trade secrets. There may also be copyrights and patents. These look good on your books.

As Professor Ron Adner of Dartmouth College's Tuck School of Business points out in his seminal book *The Wide Lens: What Successful Innovators See That Others Miss*, for an innovation to make it to market, there must be wins, or at least no negative impact, for all the stakeholders in the relevant "innovation ecosystem." In Figure 3.15 are some typical stakeholders in an innovation ecosystem. Companies in the supply chain servicing the ultimate customers (end users) are obvious, as are regulators and funding agencies. Often overlooked are opinion leaders (experts, trade publications and other traditional and social media gurus, key people in advocacy groups, etc.), industry and professional association and society officers and committee chairs or members, and key people in relevant nongovernmental organizations (e.g., the World Bank, the World Health Organization, etc.).

As you develop your R&D proposal concept for maturing the technology, you should float the concept with stakeholders to improve your chances of winning. A stakeholder table, like the one in Figure 3.15, can be made using a word processing or spreadsheet program. It allows you to quantitatively rank the support you likely will receive on a scale of more or less. The best way to determine what kind of support you will have is

Level of Commitment	People or Group						
	Supply Chain	Regulators	Opinion Leaders	Customers	Funders	NGOs	Industry Assoc.
Enthusiastic							
Helpful							
Compliant							
Hesitant							
Indifferent							
Uncooperative							
Opposed							
Hostile							

Figure 3.15 **A stakeholder table provides insight into roadblocks to commercialization of an innovation**

Source: © Foresight Science & Technology 2015.

Abbreviation: NGO, nongovernmental organization.

to call people in each stakeholder group. If the proposal concept is not receiving good support, it is better to change it before you start formally writing it.

When calling people, I use a method called "fishing." I float a general concept with the first caller. He or she bounces off of it and suggests changes. I modify my concept and float the new one with the next person. (In effect, I am using the concept as bait for the discussion. If I do not give something concrete for people to bounce off of, there often is an awkwardness as they are not clear about what I am doing and thus how to respond.) I find after about three to five calls, I start seeing convergence, meaning no one has anything new to offer. At that point, I move on to the next stakeholder group.

Methodologically, what I am doing is a takeoff on a Delphi Panel. In the Delphi method, a panel of experts receives a set of questions and sends answers to a facilitator. The facilitator summarizes them anonymously and sends them back out, together with the reasons for each answer. The experts read the response and are encouraged to revise their earlier answers in light of the replies of other panelists. Over time, there is usually a convergence. Alternatively, at some point, the facilitator cuts it off and develops what he or she feels is an acceptable set of answers. In effect, the Delphi method combines a P-Beauty Contest approach with expert interviews.

If time is limited, there are three critical stakeholders to consult: program managers at the funding agency, commercialization partners (licenses, strategic alliance partners, etc.), and the ultimate end users (the customers).

Ideally, you want to float your R&D proposal concept with the funding agencies to make sure there is interest. In the United States, it is possible to talk to program managers before a solicitation opens, not after. If they like your concept, program officers may even ask for a white paper or draft solicitation topic language. Once the solicitation is issued, no contact is permitted except through the designated contract officer in order to avoid even the appearance of impropriety.

Be aware that whatever you discuss or propose is not likely to show up verbatim in the solicitation or request for proposals. Many years ago, I was working with a small business. They had an idea for a better air circulation model relevant for weather prediction. I found the relevant program manager and the conversation went so well, he asked for a few paragraphs on their approach draft solicitation language. This was provided. A month later, when the request for proposals issued, the researcher at the small firm called me to complain his topic was not there. I got the solicitation, found the topic, and pointed it out to him. He said, "That's not my language." I responded, "Of course not. He is not going to break confidentiality and put your approach out for everyone to read. What he has done is put out a call for better air circulation models." My client wrote a proposal and won.

The views and needs of licensees and other commercialization partners (which we shall call targets) and end users can be addressed through concurrent engineering. In concurrent engineering, the end users and commercialization partners are invited to engage in discussions about new products or services from the beginning of R&D focused toward product development, rather than later in the process after the product definition is locked in. Also included are internal or contractor representatives for manufacturing, marketing and sales, and postsale customer support and maintenance. As Figure 3.16 from Wikipedia (http://en.wikipedia.org/wiki/Concurrent_engineering) highlights, concurrent engineering is a cyclical iterative process rather than a linear sequential one.

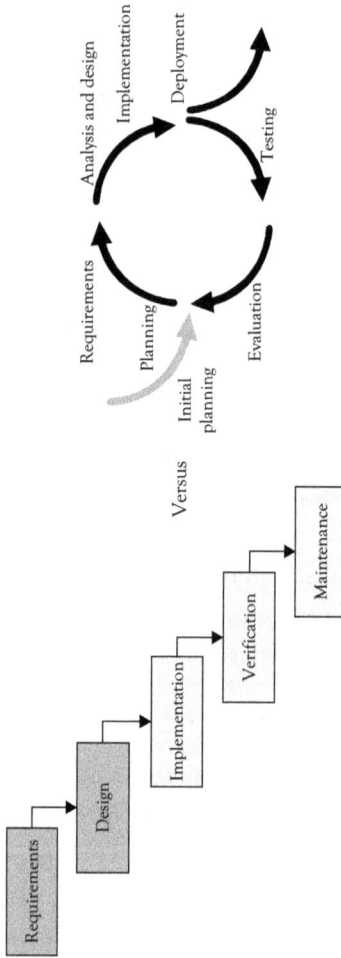

Figure 3.16 Traditional "waterfall" or sequential development method versus iterative development method in concurrent engineering

Source: Wikipedia at http://en.wikipedia.org/wiki/Concurrent_engineering

For SMEs, I recommend planning for at least two rounds (see Figure 3.17). These rounds are best conducted with everyone in one room, but web conferencing also is viable. The first round takes place early in open innovation, shortly after the acquisition of a new technology. This round focuses on getting formal advice from key people who will be involved in the downstream commercialization either as targets in the supply chain to the ultimate customers and from those customers (the end users) themselves. The goal here is to generate enough support that you can follow up afterward with the outside participants and garner letters of support for your proposal. Even better is to garner in-kind or cash match for the government or foundation money you are seeking. Among relevant in-kind support is the supply of free materials and components from targets who want to be your future vendors and commitments to participate in alpha or beta testing by customers. For potential licensees or other downstream targets, advice on transitioning into production and provision of independent test and evaluation is desirable. A match is a good sign that this technology will head to market if the funding agency puts money into the R&D. The best support is, of course, cash. It is fine if the cash is for an option to acquire all or some of the rights in the technology as it emerges from the government- or foundation-funded work.

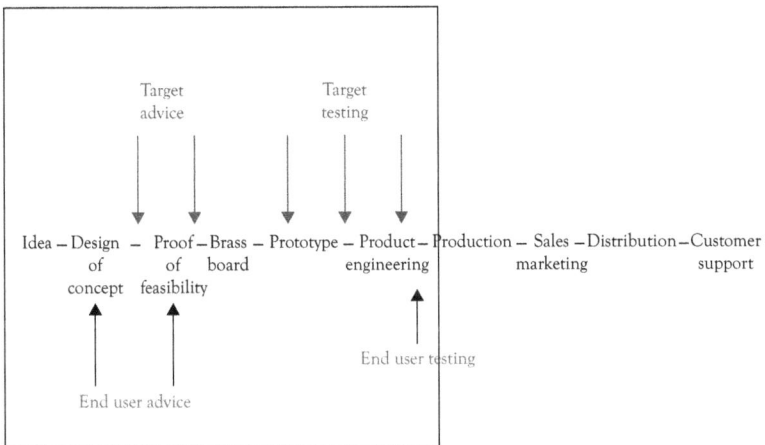

Figure 3.17 The two key phases or rounds of concurrent engineering during SME open innovation

Source: © Foresight Science & Technology 2015.

The second round takes place near the end of product engineering as you prepare to transition to production engineering and production. This is the last time it is feasible to work design modifications without significant costs. The goal here is to line up and close deals—either sales or licenses.

Of course, a critical aspect of pulling off concurrent engineering is finding the right partners. Figure 3.18 highlights what to look for in commercialization partners. The ideal partners have strong market presence and sales capability but are weaker in technology development and, if you want to produce goods as well, in manufacturing.

Planning for Transitioning

Transitioning involves moving a technology out of R&D and into production. Transitioning is a process of risk reduction and roadblock removal. First, you map out a plan for reaching the market, and then you identify all the potential risks and obstacles and remove them.

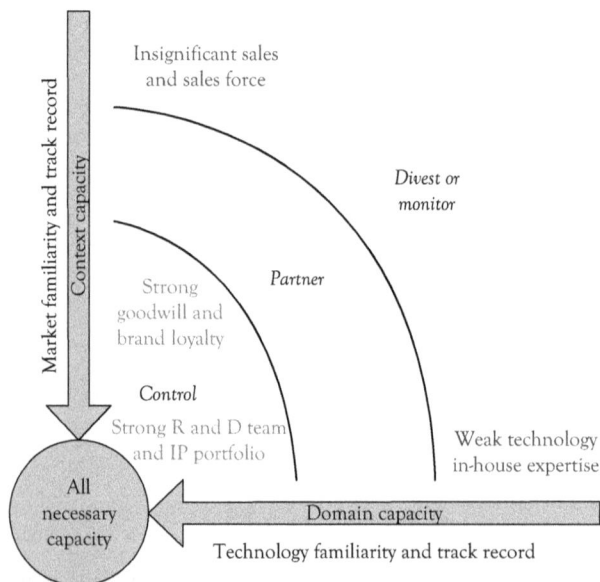

Figure 3.18 Characterizing potential partners

Source: © Foresight Science & Technology 2015.

The way to think about transitioning is to map out your current technology readiness level (TRL) and then determine what needs to be done in what order to reach the highest TRL (typically 9). Because TRLs were originally developed by U.S. government mission agencies, they need to be adapted a bit for commercial technology. Figure 3.19, from the U.S. space agency NASA, provides a hardware-based example. NASA's approach is described at www.nasa.gov/topics/aeronautics/features/trl_demystified.html

The University of Southern California's Marshall School of Business provides a set of TRLs for a variety of different technological areas at www.usc.edu/org/techalliance/pdf/CTC_TRI_Definitions-2007.pdf. You can also find discussions of TRLs for most categories of technology via web searching. A discussion on how to build your own TRL calculator is at www.dtic.mil/ndia/2003systems/nolte2.pdf

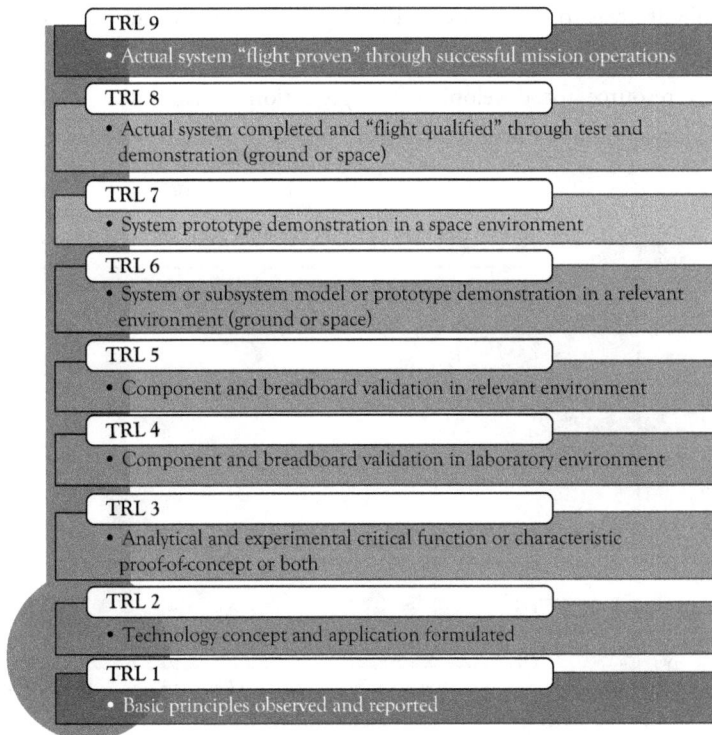

TRL 9
• Actual system "flight proven" through successful mission operations

TRL 8
• Actual system completed and "flight qualified" through test and demonstration (ground or space)

TRL 7
• System prototype demonstration in a space environment

TRL 6
• System or subsystem model or prototype demonstration in a relevant environment (ground or space)

TRL 5
• Component and breadboard validation in relevant environment

TRL 4
• Component and breadboard validation in laboratory environment

TRL 3
• Analytical and experimental critical function or characteristic proof-of-concept or both

TRL 2
• Technology concept and application formulated

TRL 1
• Basic principles observed and reported

Figure 3.19 Technology readiness levels used by NASA

Source: www.nasa.gov/content/technology-readiness-level/

Moving from one TRL to the next is a process of risk reduction. Risk has two components in transitioning. The first is delay. This slows down the time to market, thereby reducing the present value of the growth opportunity that open innovation is supposed to provide. The other is cost. Due to poor planning or unforeseen events, the transition costs more than anticipated, thereby reducing the NPV of the acquired technology. These two components are depicted in Figure 3.20. The more the potential for additional cost or delay is controlled, the lower the risk.

Building a tool like the one presented in Figure 3.21 helps focus on what risks exist and how you plan to mitigate them. Figure 3.21 is an example of a Foresight Science & Technology Transitioning Plan. It is based on extending the U.S. Defense Science Board's Willoughby Templates for transitioning from R&D to production. This example focused on transitioning a quadcopter hardware or software system for wildland fire fighting to the market. The outcome of this process is to highlight areas to emphasize in R&D proposals or in internally funded work when spinning up a technology.

A resource for developing risk reduction plans is the University of Maryland at College Park's Best Manufacturing Practices Center

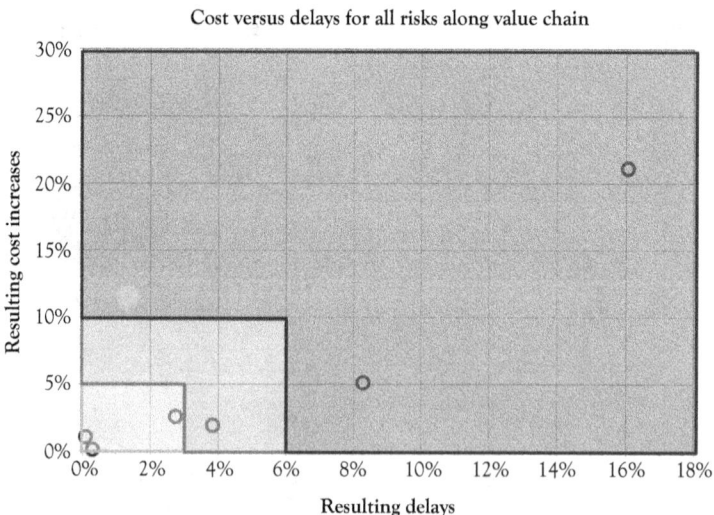

Figure 3.20 Risk is potential for unanticipated costs and delays

Source: © Foresight Science & Technology 2015.

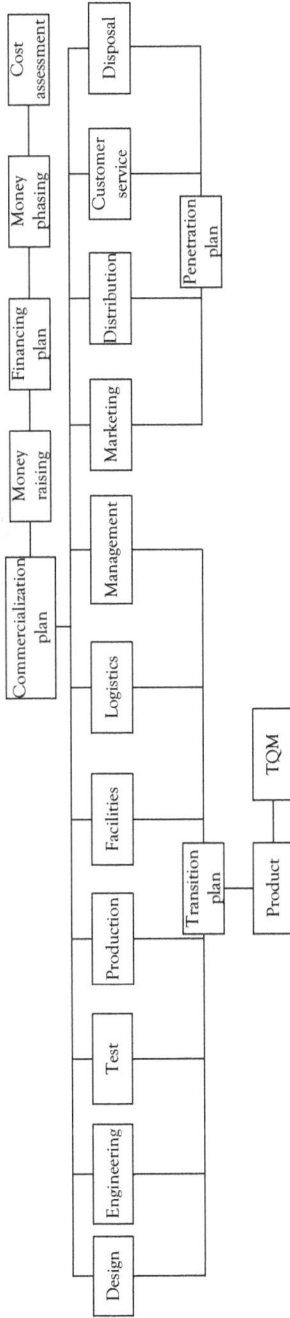

Figure 3.21 Areas of risk reduction to address in transitioning an unmanned vehicle for wildland fire fighting to the market

Source: © Foresight Science & Technology 2015.

Abbreviation: TQM, total quality management.

(www.bmpcoe.org/). The Center has a tool called TRIMS, the "Technical Risk Identification and Mitigation System," which can be used to build risk reduction models. TRIMS was used to help develop the model behind Figure 3.19. Supporting TRIMS is the Center's extensive database of risk mitigation reports and know-how. Unfortunately, TRIMS is only available to U.S. companies or "by any person or organization in support of the U.S. government, Department of Defense, or U.S. Industrial or Academic interests." TRIMS is part of a software and electronic data suite of tools called the Program Managers Workstation (PMWS).

Another factor to recognize is that TRIMS and PMWS only address the transition from R&D to production, so Foresight Science & Technology had to add all the risk reduction tasking associated with entering the market and building market share. A set of useful resources for learning about product development is published by the Product Development and Management Association. See www.pdma.org/p/cm/ld/fid=109

Planning for Exit

Exit is where you make money. Usually exit occurs in one of two ways:

1. You sell or license the technology.
2. You sell products or services based on it or incorporating it.

Doing deals is complicated and my advice is to hire a consultant to help you if you have never done a deal before. To ensure alignment of interests, consultants should have only a small up-front fee and a significant commission on success. The up-front fee is usually required to show you are serious about doing a deal. If the SME has nothing committed, there is nothing to prevent the SME from walking away from a good deal. In general, it is a wise policy to define the minimally acceptable deal up-front when you hire a consultant to help with deal-making. That keeps everyone from wasting each other's time.

The basic process for deal-making is the same for any approach. You find targets, you pitch them, listen to their responses, and, after figuring out what you want, you try to respond in ways that lead to negotiations (see Figure 3.22).

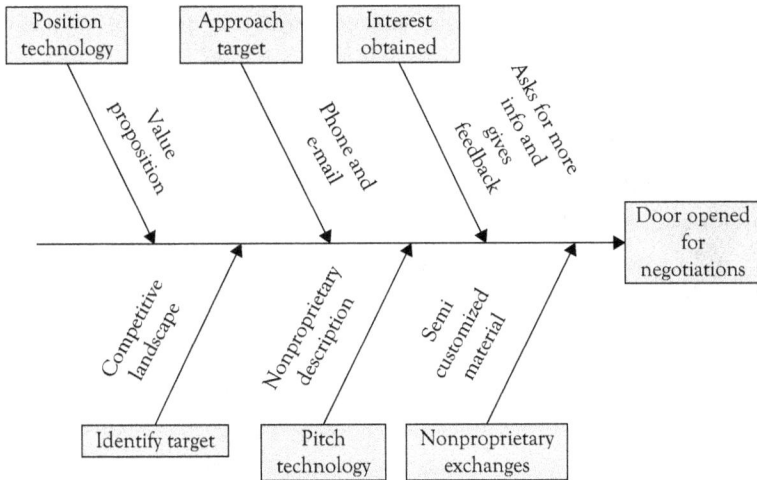

Figure 3.22 Getting to negotiations

Once the door opens for negotiations, there usually is a period of tire kicking as they make sure the technology performs as described. Once that is completed, if the target is still interested, financial terms are negotiated. If it seems like a deal is feasible, other terms are negotiated. As indicated earlier in this chapter, all terms have financial consequences and impacts, so the payments and their timing may shift somewhat as the negotiations proceed.

My recommendation for figuring out what you want in financial and other terms is to use a variant of the decision calculus described by the famous American Benjamin Franklin in his autobiography. On a spreadsheet or piece of paper, make three columns with the following headings: *Must Haves, No Ways,* and *Nice to Haves.* The must haves and the no ways provide the basis for your term sheet. As in our earlier discussion, the term sheet has to allow for convergence. As the seller, you want to sell high. Nonetheless, it is important to submit something in the "fair and reasonable" range. An outlandish offer will be rejected and cut off the possibility of negotiations.

The negotiation process is one of seeking your must haves and avoiding no ways. You use your nice to haves as trading chips. You trade them away to avoid no ways or obtain must haves. When you have the must haves and do not have any no ways, sign.

The good news is, if you have done concurrent engineering, you likely have already identified your licensee or lead customer and built relationships with the customer. That ongoing relationship should have created trust. Trust allows approaching negotiations from the perspective that you are both on the same team, trying to get this deal past whoever must sign off for both parties.

When negotiating, remember what Ben Franklin said in the *Poor Richard's Almanack*: "Pride is as loud a beggar as need and a good deal more saucy." In our context, what that means is the parties to a deal always have three choices—do it, wait or stall or both, or walk away. Your job is to understand what they need to sign a deal and to help them either get it or find a way to do the deal without it. That means you cannot take a no as *no* unless the other party says, "Go away and do not darken my door again." No is simply an opening for a conversation. You want to come away from this conversation understanding the following:

- Do you correctly understand why the technology is attractive?
- What is the decision process and who else is involved in what roles or functions?
- How long does the decision process take?
- What criteria will be important and why?
- What information will they want?
- What kind of deals have they signed in the past and what do they prefer?
- Who is (are) the decision maker(s)?
- What other insights do they have that can make the negotiations smoother and quicker?

Usually the problems go back to something Franklin's Poor Richard also said: "It is hard for an empty bag to stand upright." What that means is everyone has to make money and be better off after the deal than before. Otherwise, why do it?

When deals make good business sense, they are self-enforcing. Good business sense results when there are three things:

1. Net positive cash flow for all parties
2. A fair allocation of cash flow (the revenues from sales or gross profit to each party are proportional to value contributed)
3. Both carrots and sticks for both parties in the clauses of the agreement

Net positive cash flow has to take into account that cash today is worth more than cash tomorrow due to discounting. Therefore, the total anticipated revenues to the seller should lower where there are one-time up-front cash payments than where running royalties are used. That is because of the risk that the downstream payments may never materialize.

Because deals involve managing risk, another principle is that the more risk a party bears, the more upside cash flow potential it deserves. The objective in negotiations is to allocate risk to the party able to control it or bear it. Finally, if the seller is deferring revenue, milestone payments and penalties for missing milestones are used to make the deal "fair" for the seller.

Closing Thoughts

Using technology transfer as an SME, the open innovation method can be summarized using three quotes:

- "Nothing happens without a sale," David Speser, chairman, Foresight Science & Technology Inc. (and my father).

The whole reason for engaging in this process is to sell things profitably. So at each step, ask yourself, "Is doing this making it easier or harder to sell something profitably?" If the answer is harder, do not do it. This principle applies to discrete tasks in open innovation and to engaging in technology transfer in the first place. Technology transfer involves a lot of work. It has real and significant transactions costs.

- "If opportunity doesn't knock, build a door," Milton Berle, vaudeville comedian.

Finding technologies, spinning them up, and flipping them is at the heart of open innovation. In technology transfer, the technologies come from research institutions and they are sold directly to the end users or flipped to companies in a supply chain selling to those end users. Technology transfer is still a relatively young field. It did not exist until after World War II. So the pathways for doing it are still evolving and being worked out. Complicating things is the fact that there is competition for whatever good an SME hopes to introduce to the market or license at the end of its open innovation process. The owners of competing technology would prefer that the SME not succeed. It is up to the SME to make it happen despite their objections and hindrance. To do that, the SME has to build a door into a relevant supply chain, just as it has to build a door into the institutions with the technology. If it wants a subsidy for spinning up the technology, it also has to build a door to the funding agencies. Building doors involves market research. But more importantly, it involves picking up the phone and talking to people or going to visit them. It is people who shake hands and sign contracts and licenses. If you do not get to know them, it is hard to get a deal.

- "A well-defined imagination is the source of great deeds,"
  Chinese fortune cookie.

I have presented an approach for doing technology transfer. While the tasks that need to be accomplished can be relatively well defined, the order in which they are done and the ones that are necessary are not set in stone. Flexibility is important.

CHAPTER 4

The Power of "Crowdsolving"

Adriano La Vopa

Introduction

Like open innovation, crowdsourcing has become a buzzword. Especially for small and medium enterprises (SMEs), where surplus cash is often negligible, we believe that when a company approaches the crowd, it should be done in a careful and structured way. The risk of doing crowdsourcing without the correct "preparation" is a recipe for dramatic failure. It is imperative to have a clear idea on what to ask the crowd and then determine which is the best "crowd" to approach and how to get their attention.

Crowdsourcing overlaps with some other open innovation approaches, like technology scouting or cocreation with lead users, to mention only two. Indeed, it is difficult to position crowdsourcing in a separate frame from other approaches. The use of the crowd is already an indication that the company is open and that is seeking solutions provided by people outside its own supply chain (see Figure 4.1).

As shown in the picture, the search for solutions via the crowd can be used in a variety of contexts. Usually, the crowd is engaged in one of two different ways: the first is by launching a contest and the other is by opening a challenge. Since the words contest and challenge are synonyms, it is important to explain how we understand them.

A contest is usually initiated to attract new ideas or designs, or to call for cocreation of new concepts. A fun example is the National Aeronautics and Space Administration (NASA) Goddard Space Flight Center's Optimus Prime Spinoff Challenge where precollegiate students propose new products that leverage space technology to solve problems on earth

Open innovation umbrella

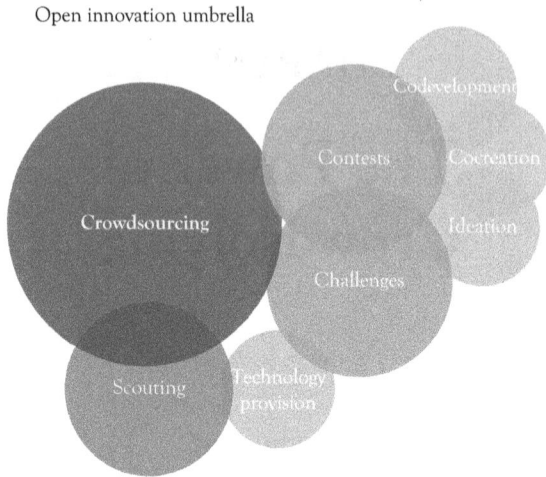

Figure 4.1 Crowdsourcing. Crowdsourcing follows the open innovation paradigm and is under its umbrella but overlaps with other methods covered in it

(see http://ipp.gsfc.nasa.gov/optimus/). In a contest, a company usually posts a need to be addressed, a time frame for submission of ideas, and, in most of the cases, there is a selection process that leads to rewarding the winner with a prize. The contestants usually are asked to submit their ideas in a "conceptual" way. For instance, a design contest typically asks for submissions of visual material (three-dimensional [3D] videos, sketches, storybooks, drawings, etc.), since the need of the company could be to look for a new concept of their product or a totally new product they never thought about. The NASA Optimus Prime Spinoff Challenge has the children make videos illustrating the use of the product.

A challenge is something more elaborate, where the crowd is called to participate with ideas that are mainly solutions to a problem that the company has defined. In a challenge, the company posts its own need, which is essentially a problem that could not be fixed internally, and then the call is open to the crowd. The need may be posted on its own portal or that of an intermediary. It can be a company-specific portal or one shared with other entities, such as http://Launch.org. Here the contributors submit more elaborated ideas, in many cases, a proof of concept involving technologies that are protected by patent, copyright, mask, or other intellectual property (IP) rights. A challenge could be granted with some prizes, awards, or recognitions, or, in some cases, the possibility to work with the company to develop the winning solution. A challenge foresees activities of problem solving, cocreation, and codevelopment of solutions for a specific problem. In the following, we use the example of an SME in the injection molding business, which has encountered a problem during product development. It poses a challenge on their portal for a crowd of innovative suppliers to respond to. When a solution emerges, it is adopted and immediately used by the company.

Although the difference may seem minor, this brief explanation highlights that crowdsourcing, as a method of open innovation, requires attention to objectives and requirements, who the crowd is, how they will be approached, and how they will be rewarded. In this chapter, we guide you through how to think about crowdsourcing. Along the way, we provide some examples on how the potential of the crowd can be used.

Specifically, for SMEs looking for ideas and advice (or money) from the crowd, we believe the approach to follow is "crowdsolving." The reason for this rewording is because you want to ask the crowd to solve *your* problems. Going to the crowd can provide access to new knowledge and expertise that can be applied by SMEs to come up with the right solutions. Crowdsolving should be the overriding concern when using crowdsourcing.

In this chapter, we explore using crowds. Suggestions on how to determine what needs are appropriate to take to the crowd are provided as well as advice on how to define them and guiding templates to ensure you capture all the essential parts of the process. In addition, we discuss what to do when solutions start coming in. Here, we examine how to deal with some of the trickier parts of the process: the IP, the risks involved, the roles to give to contributors, and how to motivate and involve them effectively.

Defining Crowdsourcing

Crowdsourcing, like most of the methodologies commonly used within open innovation, is a way of exploiting the knowledge of the crowd. Like open innovation in general, crowdsourcing was originally a process used primarily by large companies. Today, SMEs, including start-ups, exploit it.

The first use of the term crowdsourcing was in an article from Jeff Howe in *Wired* magazine[1] back in 2006. He said, "The new pool of cheap labor: everyday people using their spare cycles to create content, solve problems, even do corporate R&D." His article proposed for the first time a reasoned analysis on some successful examples from a crowd of unusual contributors. iStockPhoto, InnoCentive, NineSigma, and Mechanical Turk are some of the examples he mentioned. What his analysis pointed out was the economic benefits engaging with a crowd of people that could provide extremely competitive solutions to problems. Compared to hiring professional consultants and researchers, he pointed out that the crowd is a "cheap labor" force. After this first publication on the subject of crowdsourcing, many others followed, addressing the different definitions, the motivations pushing individuals, the "types" of such individuals, and, of course, the different ways of managing this huge innovative power.

Nowadays, it is common to read in both the scholarly and popular press and blogs that most innovation comes from customers and consumers who are seeking more performance, better quality-price ratios, better product features and functionality, and so forth. Companies that listen to customers and consumers use this feedback to improve their existing products and create new ones. More and more companies are claiming to be "consumer (or customer) centric," and indeed they are. It does not really matter if the business is B2B, B2C, or B2B2C. Today's global economy is driven by innovation, and an SME that ignores the harsh reality of product life cycles has a hard time surviving.

While the length of product life cycles and the diversity of products offered varies by industry, in innovation-driven economies, failure to innovate effectively and cost efficiently can dramatically jeopardize an SME's competitiveness. In both large companies and SMEs, there is constant pressure to come up with new brilliant ideas that can be translated into blockbuster products—or at least solid performers. Yet, especially in SMEs with a small or no research and development (R&D) department, these new product ideas can be hard to discover. Everyone is too

[1] Howe, J. 2006. "The Rise of Crowdsourcing." *Wired*, January 06, 2006. www.wired.com/2006/06/crowds/

busy with the day-to-day operations, and the need to support day-to-day operations diverts even future-focused R&D. R&D can also be too biased by their technical domain. Despite its best efforts, lack of time, lack of money, and lack of broad-ranging technical expertise can make it hard to find the right solution to problems in current operations, let alone develop new products. These are common issues for any company, of any size, and with any type of capital reserves and investment raising capabilities. So the question becomes: What to do then?

Clearly, one possible answer is crowdsourcing. If we simply divide the word in two, it is clear the meaning of crowdsourcing is that someone gets something from the contributions of a group of individuals in reply to the request by that someone. Thus, in order for an SME to use this method, it has to determine the type of source, the type of crowd, and the approach (Figure 4.2) that best fits the problems it would solve or the questions it would answer.

Crowdsourcing is sometimes thought of as rainmaking for the company using it. If we follow this metaphor, we can assume that the crowd is like a cloud comprising a group of individuals who are sharing the same interests, passions, and, perhaps, the same professions. The targeted crowd is a *community* of people who should be willing to contribute to your addressing need because of their own interests. However, just who the crowd actually is when you do crowdsource is usually highly uncertain. It is difficult to foresee who will be in the crowd when an open request is made to source something—especially when using the Internet.

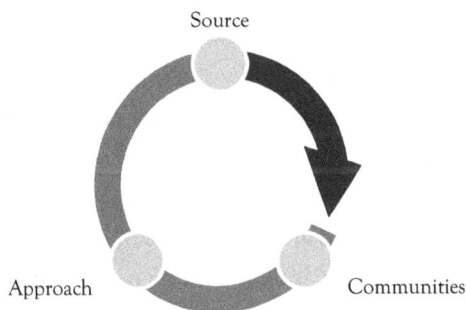

Figure 4.2 Crowdsourcing cycle. When a company decides to challenge the crowd, it is important to structure the right approach and address the right community for heading to the right source

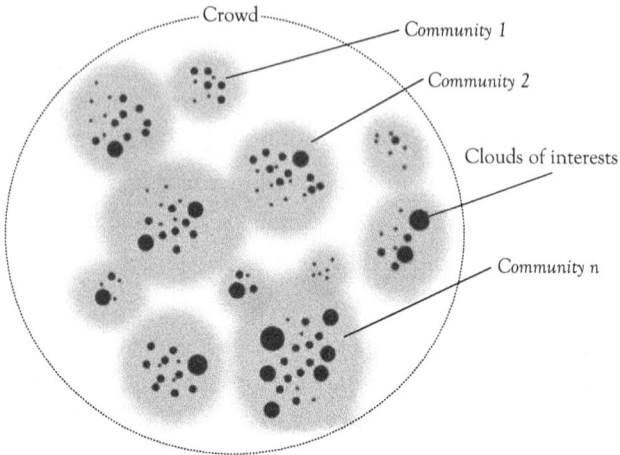

Figure 4.3 Types of communities and density (clouds) of participants according to their interests

Thus, on one side we have the defined cluster, or group, of contributors we would like to tap, while on the other, we have a larger undefined group that will see the request. We cannot usually be totally clear in advance from where replies will come. Indeed, part of the reason for crowdsourcing is we want this element of serendipity. The crowd is like a cloudy sky where inner darker clouds (groups with known interests we want to tap) are present amid a sky of gray and white clouds (diverse groups with varying interests); Figure 4.3 depicts this metaphor. Having this picture in mind, it is clear that crowdsourcing brings along an uncertainty as to whether it will rain or not and if so, from where.

The challenge becomes to find a path and approach that focuses on the targeted crowd (the right inner cloud of interests in our metaphor) in order to tap the best individuals to help us with our specific sourcing search (Figure 4.4). The solution is to use communication channels already monitored by the desired groups in our approach. If an SME is looking for software, it reaches out through blogs, trade press, newsletters, LinkedIn groups, and so on, and crowdsourcing sites that are monitored by programmers. If an SME is looking for a new coating, it reaches out through channels monitored by chemists and materials scientists. This tactic works, because individuals already are naturally clustered into communities (clouds) of interest.

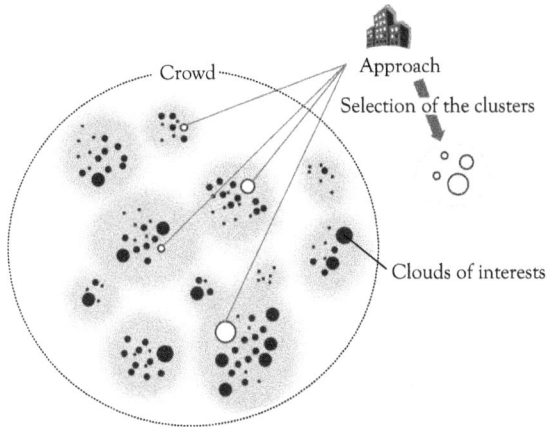

Figure 4.4 Selecting the right clusters, or the right clouds of interests, is important to approach the right source

The channel is only one part of the approach. The other parts are the message and the motivation.

Borrowing from the two main typical management approaches, top-down and the bottom-up, we can address how to structure these in crowdsourcing.

The Top-Down Approach

The top-down approach implies that a clear need definition comes directly from the top (in crowdsourcing is usually the company making the request). This request is translated and broken down into the lingo of the community whose advice is being sought. The same request can give birth to a myriad of targeted messages depending on the diversity of the crowd being sourced. What does not vary across messages is the underlying specifications and constraints that define an acceptable solution. The top-down approach emphasizes that it is the SME that drives the request or the challenge, and that to respond, a contributor must be bound by this request and its specifications. Figure 4.5 depicts this approach.

A challenge in a top-down approach is to provide an incentive for responding that cuts across various communities, as it is impossible to ensure that a member of one community may not see a message directed to another community. For example, if an SME could target only

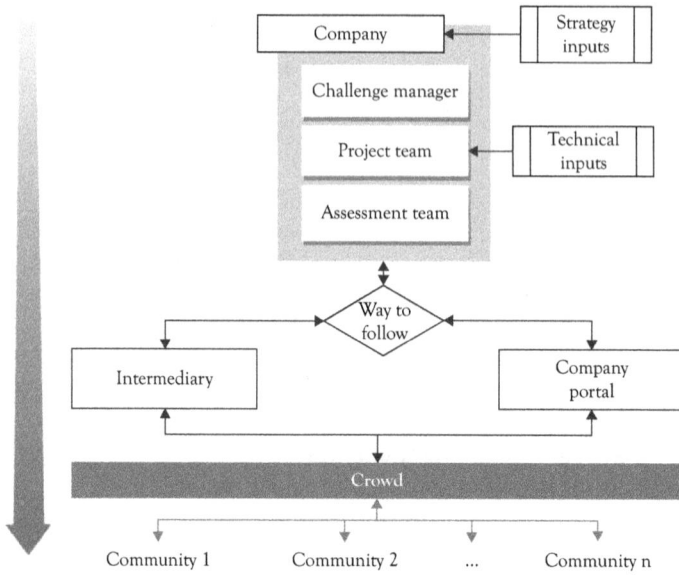

Figure 4.5 Top-down approach

graduating college students, a job might be a good incentive. But a job would not be much of an incentive for a retiree. This potential diversity of motivations across communities is probably the reason monetary prizes or rewards and public recognition are among the primary incentives used to stimulate responses when crowdsourcing ideas. (Crowdsourcing investments rely on different motivations, of course. As previously noted, like the channel, both the message and the motivation have to be carefully considered when planning the approach.)

Use of Intermediaries

Consider, for instance, a company producing connectors for a customer that sells equipment to electric power grid operators. This company is a medium enterprise with a couple of hundred employees and a turnover of about $20 million. The R&D department consists of a number of engineers and designers who are developing, designing, and testing the new connectors. The firm's marketing director comes to the head of R&D with a new interesting idea captured in a discussion with their main customer.

The idea is to create a connected connector, which is a connector that has the ability to measure and transmit data on the energy consumption occurring at a specific node of a power line. The firm's "customer-driven" management immediately approves this project. The challenge for R&D is to create the product. The head of R&D has two choices: develop the connectivity system in-house or develop the connectivity system by using external resources. Assume this SME does not have all the necessary capabilities in-house. For the head of R&D, it makes sense to explore the open innovation option before incurring the costs of acquiring new capabilities to create the product from scratch. How does the firm do that?

A possible option is to use one of the many service providers, or intermediaries, that help companies in reaching a wide network of solvers. Intermediaries are service providers who can help define and (and sometimes or, depending on their services) implement the approach in exchange for fees. Usually, such intermediaries are companies that have either a network of a wide range of solution providers or a publically accessible portal where they collect different problems provided by customers (the SME in this case).

In the former case, the intermediary reaches out to its network in order to discover solution providers. It may also send messages through channels frequented by people likely to have, or be able to develop at a moderate cost, solutions. It reviews replies it receives for compliance with the requirements of the SME client and forwards the ones that meet those requirements to the client.

In the latter case, the intermediary posts the request on its own portal. These portals may be open to all or only accessible after registration and possibly some due diligence on the registrant. Problem solvers subscribing to such portals may get newsletters or rich site summary (RSS) feeds on the latest problems posted. Distinct from the prior intermediary who reaches out broadly, this one uses a preexisting network of solvers that grows and shrinks over time depending on who registers or hits the portal. The problems of the SME could be addressed to anyone in this network.

A very important step for an SME using either kind of service is to be very clear on its needs and requirements. Good intermediaries will help their customers to create a specific proposal consisting of a clear problem statement, clear metrics for acceptable solutions, and the incentives for providing solutions. Once the proposal is clear, the project is started and outreach occurs or a post added to the portal. The problem is now out there and whoever wants to participate, can propose a solution. At the SME, the R&D department can gather the ideas solicited, review them, and select the best ones to be further explored, leading to development of their connector system.

It is critical to emphasize that posting a request, unless it is carefully worded, may be making a contract offer. If someone meets the requirements, and responds, the SME may find that under contract law, the responding party has accepted the offer and the SME is now legally bound to pay (or provide whatever incentive is proposed) for the solution. For this reason, a lawyer needs to review what is being sent out to solicit responses. The good news is that once a "safe" boilerplate is created that clearly states the request is not a legally binding offer but merely an exploration of options, it can be used by the SME to make a variety of requests. If the intermediary insists the SME use its template, the SME's lawyer, in advance of any dissemination or posting of the request, should review it.

The aforementioned scenario is typical of when a company does not want to run this activity on their own, and for this reason, they decide to pay for an intermediary to do so for them. This approach has pros and cons. It is convenient when the company is inexperienced in crowdsourcing and advantageous when the company does not want their name to be disclosed. On the other hand, the use of intermediaries almost always means they have to pay something. For the SME, the question is whether the benefits gained are worth the cost. That depends on more than the price paid. It also depends on the quality of the work the intermediary does. Since crowdsourcing is a growing field, the number of such organizations is growing fast. It is now possible to find a wide range of services offered at a wide range of prices. We stress that, at present, very few intermediaries specialize in providing services to small and medium-sized companies. As with any vendor, intermediaries can be very expensive, particularly if the wrong ones are chosen, so conduct your due diligence before retaining one.

Use of a Company-Owned Portal

A company that operates in the injection-molding machine sector has a very competent R&D department of 25 engineers. A project is developing a new machine that will inject recently developed polymers into the same molds currently used by their customers to make multicomponent products. Unfortunately, R&D has hit a problem as the hot chambers for injecting the material clog if the viscosity of the material is not controlled very precisely. Indeed the viscosity "window" is so narrow that the new polymers consistently overcome the thresholds and clog the injector. Without a solution, this problem will derail the entire project. Despite their best efforts, the R&D department is not yet able to provide a feasible, cost-efficient solution. The management is worried about the cost of this project and foresees serious problems if they were to the launch production of this new machine on schedule.

The SME's core expertise is in assembling the injection-molding machine and developing the software that controls it. The parts and components they use come from suppliers. The vice president of Operations has read about how the big auto and aerospace companies have been forcing R&D and innovation down the supply chain onto their vendors. Before abandoning the project, the management decides to try this approach and challenge their vendors to come up with a solution. (Up until now, these vendors have only been suppliers. They know nothing about this new R&D program.)

The management posts a challenge to all their suppliers on a password-protected section of their intranet portal. They also send the challenge to some potential new vendors. The prize is a contract. Vendors and potential vendors have one month to submit their solutions. The challenge in not advertised on social media or trade publications, as the management does not want to telegraph this initiative to their competition. To encourage creativity by current vendors, everyone who is receiving the challenge is identified on the portal. The community of parts and components suppliers that comprise this crowd starts submitting solutions and new ideas. At the closure of the challenge, the company gathers many solutions to the problem and decides to implement a solution provided from two suppliers that codeveloped it.

In this case, the company has used their own means to advertise their needs and to mobilize their supply base, the latter responding in a very positive way and feeling part of the innovation process. This activity brought an immediately implementable solution, due to the fact that the company worked with their suppliers and other handpicked vendors, which meant working with a pool of experts who already know the business and the product. At the same time, the resources invested in all the process were paid back handsomely by the "fully packed" solution. Our SME has hit big by taking a risk.

Summary of Top-Down Approach

Top-down approaches work best where there is a specific problem your company is trying to solve. Usually this approach makes the most sense for solving process technology problems or for finding incremental product innovations. The two examples demonstrate it is possible either to use unrestricted crowds to do top-down open innovation or to limit the sourcing to a small select group. Regardless, top-down crowdsourcing only works where the SME is clear about the problem to be solved or product to be developed and can provide to the crowd what makes a solution feasible and cost-efficient (in the following figures you will see a simple chart which can be used to guide your company in tackling and defining a "needs proposal").

The Bottom-Up Approach

The bottom-up approach (Figure 4.6) involves a different flow of contributions and typically works best when the company has a goal or objective in mind but not a specific problem. An example is the Ansari X PRIZE for the first nongovernment organization to launch a reusable manned spacecraft into space twice within two weeks. For SMEs, bottom-up open innovation provides a way to tap the external world in order to get a clearer understanding of opportunities in the market and develop products addressing those needs. As Eric von Hippel pointed out in his book on innovation communities, products like UNIX and the windsurf board grew out of collaboration with a community (a crowd). As the technology

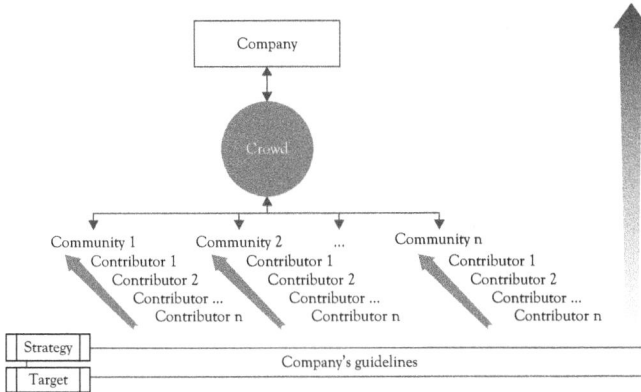

Figure 4.6 Bottom-up approach

matured, one group of contributors realized they could build a company (e.g., Red Hat for UNIX) by capturing the open source innovations and wrapping them with a service and support organization. For an SME using a bottom-up approach, the objective is to define the market and a pathway and then encourage others to build upon it in exchange for either rights in or free or low-cost use of the resulting product.

Use of Your Own Network

Consider an SME that operates in the furniture business. The firm has about 150 employees and a turnover of about $20 million. Our SME is proud to be a customer-centric company. Indeed, acting in the B2C environment, they have to be very attentive to the trends of fashion, to the different regional preferences where they sell their products, to the different offerings of competitors, and, of course, to the range of tastes of their customers. Although such a company has a strong department of designers, engineers, and technicians who are capable of coming up with extremely good ideas, in 2007, they saw a downturn of about 15 percent in their profits. After some analysis of the causes of the downturn, they realized it was not enough to blame the global recession as there were bright spots in Asian and other emerging markets that they had failed to exploit. Facing this challenge head-on, the company decided to invest in creating their own network of sales advocates and advisors. To build this network, they reached out to customers, designers, architects, journalists, and others who played important roles in furniture markets around the world. They posted their newsfeed's existence to social media as well as the traditional trade press and blogs. For anyone who registered, they offered a free subscription to the company's internal synopsis of each day's news about the furniture business, design trends, and new or improved materials for furniture. By doing so, in a very short time, the company had gathered a substantial crowd, which was interested in innovative ideas for furniture. By adding incentives (primarily recognition and honors) for posting to their news and comment feed, they created a crowd that was very participative and extremely keen to compete on new product idea generation.

In this bottom-up approach, the company can add its own posts and news to "indicate the way" to their crowd. By adding permissioning to their blog or newsfeed, they can allow employees to make comments that are not seen by nonemployees. Thus, internal and external contributors belong to the same cloud, even though there are different subcommunities within that cloud

Bottom-up innovation has both pros and cons.

By opening up, the company enhances its goodwill and reputation as an innovation leader in the industry. It can encourage external people to submit their product ideas and suggestions. By being more open and transparent to customers, it advertises that it wants to hear their voice and demonstrates their voice is really heard and put into practice. It can tap into the collective wisdom and creativity of the crowd to develop ways to respond to posted suggestions for products and product improvements.

On the contrary, opening up carries risks because the company is more exposed to external parties. Competitors could also use the discussion on its portal to develop better products that respond to consumer preferences.

What this discussion highlights is that open innovation cannot be practiced without thinking about the other activities and capabilities of the company. Rapid prototyping, agile manufacturing, and lean Six Sigma are examples of tools that provide means to rapidly identify and respond to emerging consumer trends and product suggestions. Rapid product development enables leveraging opportunities from open innovation before your competitors, providing the benefits of first mover advantages. The openness of the company and the potentials of this innovative exercise revealed that being open is not always a drawback. With some planning and coinvestment in product development, manufacturing, and sales, it can create more interest and enthusiasm in the crowd to work with, and buy from, your company instead of your competitors.

Create, Develop, and Sell

What the World Wide Web has done is create opportunities for asynchronous collaboration between people who will never meet face-to-face. What is fascinating for SMEs interested in open innovation is the affordability of the use of portals. Any company can use off the shelf software to set up their own open innovation portal to gather and improve on ideas from the crowd until they become winners.

The way these portals work is quite simple and reminiscent of the early years of software user group meetings. People interested in the topic register for access, or the portal provides open access to all. (We prefer registration as they also collect contact information for alpha and beta testers and lead customers.) A participant submits an idea. This idea is visible to the whole community subscribed to, or viewing, the portal. The community reviews the idea and proposes new further improvements to the idea, where needed. In this way, the idea is enhanced during its life on the portal. A similar dynamic is seen on Wikipedia; only there, it is articles being proposed and the content of those articles that is being improved.

To rank product ideas, voting can be introduced. People vote for the ideas they like. Reviews can also act as a surrogate for voting. In effect, the way ranking works is similar to some movie review portals, like Rotten Tomatoes (www.rottentomatoes.com), travel portals like Trip Advisor (www.TripAdvisor.com), or answer portals like Answers (www.answers.com/). Product idea portals can help identify which ideas have a good chance of finding market traction. Those ideas garnering the most interest are reviewed and improved. They are refined until they reach a definition that is implementable. At that time, the SME owning the portal can capture the ones it likes and productize them internally for sale. In short, collaboration portals provide a simple way to leverage a crowd so it supports product development.

There are now several examples of open portals for gathering product ideas from the crowd. Many of these go further than collaboration and add deal-making. The idea can either be posted with a given price for its sale (with implementation) or with an auction. We do not describe further how companies are doing this, because the literature is pretty copious and easy to get, but a few easy links are reported here for reference:

A portal where artists, designers, and creatives could post their own designs and be voted by the crowd as well as sell their own T-shirts	www.threadless.com/
A portal where any inventor can post ideas, which are reviewed by peers, improved, and sold via the portal. Some big companies also look at this portal to invest in interesting ideas	www.quirky.com/invent
A portal where any inventor and creatives could post their ideas and further improve them, with the crowd participating, on the portal	https://cuusoo.com/

These three, as well as many others, are all examples for small companies interested in developing a winning crowdsourcing platform. It is good to mention, although more details emerge in the course of this chapter, that contributors who provide winning ideas should be able to benefit from them, maybe by getting a certain percentage of the sales, a royalty, or even an opportunity to comarket products of their own by giving a percentage of the sales price to the platform providers in a manner analogous to eBay (www.e-bay.com).

The Nuts and Bolts of Conducting Crowdsourcing

We now turn to the nuts and bolts of doing crowdsourcing. There are three main steps: defining the needs, conducting outreach, and assessing the solutions.

Defining the Needs

Let us start by stating this is the most difficult part of the process. It is notorious that many companies face problems in stating their problems. A nice pun, but it is actually true that defining a crowdsourcing problem is very difficult because the definition has to focus on what is an acceptable solution. The challenge is to focus on what is desired, not how it should be done.

It could seem trivial to write a need, but our experience actually shows the opposite. Most of the time, those who define a need in a company are typically the employees of the company. When people close to a problem define it, there is a degree of bias introduced into the description of the problem. Why? Simply because these people involved in the business are too close to the problem and too imbued with the internal company jargon and acronyms. On the one hand, they take things for granted that outsiders to the company may not know. On the other hand, their descriptions may reflect blinders that prevent them from seeing less obvious solutions. A quick test as to whether this insularity is occurring is to ask some of their colleagues on another floor or from another department how they understand the problem described. If it is different, there is a problem. A better test is to present the problem definition to a small group of outsiders and ask them to state it in their own words. If you agree that they correctly understand it, consider using their language for the description rather than your own. External facilitators can be helpful as well. The facilitator can be a consultant or a colleague from another team. He or she should be asked to participate in the problem definition with the mandate to ask questions when he or she does not understand what the other participants are discussing.

Having said that, what is desired has to be broken down into two elements. The first element is metrics such as engineering performance parameters and price. These have to be presented without the use of jargon since, as we discussed in the preceding, we cannot assume everyone reading the problem description will know the same lingo—or, for that matter, be a native speaker of the same language. The other element is the constraints on an acceptable solution. If a power meter is going to be used in a rural area subject to outages from trees falling on lines during storms, the meter has to be able to handle the anticipated fluctuations in the amount of power being transmitted and the harmonics in the line. The accuracy and target cost for the solution are not sufficient to define what is being sought.

We note that the downstream assessment of replies and selection of winners will be better and easier if the metrics for selection are well defined up-front. These criteria are strictly dependent on the needs of the company, so the likelihood of finding a solution for the needs will be improved if the metrics for selecting winners are determined as part of the solicitation development. It is vital they are aligned with the problem statement and specifications provided in the challenge or contest, which are then captured in the solicitation. Beware of using only general criteria, as these do not provide enough specificity to drive a selection process. At the same time, not all the specific criteria need to be disclosed as that may have adverse competitive ramifications since it tips your hand about the specifics of your future products. The balance between general and specific is as much a matter of art as of science.

For guidance on how to develop your metrics, we recommend using the same methods applied to create balanced scorecards. Essentially, you determine what is important to you, then you develop ways of measuring progress toward that. These individual metrics are then combined into more general categories, which also have measurement schema. For example, electricity meters provided by utilities have a kilowatt-per-hour measurement. When the meter is on a house that has a solar installation, there is a cost per kilowatt-hour measurement that can be positive or negative depending on how much power is used. Cost per kilowatt-hour is a general metric that combines metrics for consumption, production, and cost of electricity. The solicitation may only disclose that what is sought is a way to minimize cost per kilowatt-hour for the homeowner. Alternatively, it may disclose that what is sought is a way to increase production without affecting consumption. What metrics are used depend on what kinds of solutions are preferred from crowdsourcing and how much weeding of responses the company wants to engage in.

A Process for Defining the Needs

We recommend a four-step process to define the problem for crowd-sourcing. This process should focus on filling in a form, such as the one presented in Figure 4.7.

STRATEGIC ROADMAP HIGHLIGHTS	RESOURCES SUMMARY
<Describe the driving strategic highlights for searching for a solution>	**Budget:** <capture the total budget needed for this search> **Timeline:** <define the time for the search> **Team (FTE):** <define the total needed FTE> **SPONSORS:** <list the executive or management sponsors of this search>

NEEDS

Problem statement		Technology domain	Technology maturity
<Define clearly what is the problem to be solved>		<Define in which domain you expect to find the technology>	<Define which maturity of the technology you are aiming for>

Technical criteria	Feasibility criteria	Known solutions	IP status and listing
<List the criteria of the search>	<List the feasibility criteria of the search>	<List the solutions you already tried or know, to not get doubles>	<Define the IP status (no IP, pending, IP protected, etc) and list the patent you already know>

FINANCIALS	SERVICE	TEAM	RESULTS
Total investment	**Insourcing**	**Project team**	**Top 3 solutions**
<Capture the total investment for the search of the solution>	<Describe if you are using internal esource>	<List team members and functions>	<List the main three potential solutions>
Man hours	**Outsourcing**	**Assessment team**	**Reasons for selection**
<Capture the total or detailed man hours>	<Describe if you are outsourcing the solution souing>	<List who is going to assess and review the solutions>	<List the main reasons for selecting such solutions>
Internal services	**Consultancy**	**Point of contact**	**Impact**
<Capture the total investment in internal services>	<Describe you are using consultancy services>	<List the point of contact with their functions and roles>	<Describe the main impact on the issue to be solved>

Figure 4.7 Needs form

Abbreviation: FTE, full-time equivalent.

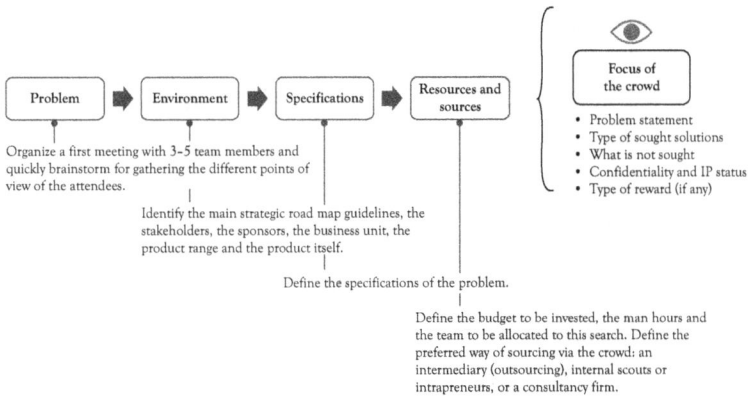

Problem → Environment → Specifications → Resources and sources

Focus of the crowd
- Problem statement
- Type of sought solutions
- What is not sought
- Confidentiality and IP status
- Type of reward (if any)

Organize a first meeting with 3–5 team members and quickly brainstorm for gathering the different points of view of the attendees.

Identify the main strategic road map guidelines, the stakeholders, the sponsors, the business unit, the product range and the product itself.

Define the specifications of the problem.

Define the budget to be invested, the man hours and the team to be allocated to this search. Define the preferred way of sourcing via the crowd: an intermediary (outsourcing), internal scouts or intrapreneurs, or a consultancy firm.

Figure 4.8 Step-by-step approach for thoroughly describing a company's needs

A systematic process should be used to define the needs a company wants to address through crowdsourcing. We present one such process in Figure 4.8. It uses the form to guide four discrete sets of activities.

Step 1 (Problem): Organize a first meeting with three to five team members and quickly brainstorm the problem definition. The objective here is to gather the different points of view of the attendees. Brainstorming is focused on filling in part A of the form in Figure 4.9. It is vital to ensure all the required data are addressed during this exercise. This brainstorming should take no more than half an hour; otherwise, you tend to get caught in a loop where people say the same thing in different ways. All the points of view shall be captured using a whiteboard or flip chart so the comments are visible to everybody in the meeting. For this activity, we discourage the use of post-its since they are simply hard to read unless you are close to them. The outcome should be a verbal description of what is being sought.

Step 2 (Internal environment): Next, the meeting focuses on identifying the context, which defines constraints on what is an acceptable solution and the metrics used to identify a successful solution. The primary input to this step is the company's strategic plan and any relevant roadmaps it has developed. The next input is the stakeholders, sponsors, and business unit(s) that will be involved and the product family and product line where the solution will fit or be applied. The final input is the sales goals, cost of goods sold to targets, and hurdle rate or cost parameters for the solution itself. (These are in part B of the template.)

Step 3 (Specifications): The last part of the meeting focuses on defining the engineering and other performance, ease-of-use, and price specifications that constitute an acceptable solution (part C).
Once the problem statement is drafted, circulate it to the whole team and to your "tester," in order to collect remarks, additions, concerns, and improvements. Refine the problem statement and iterate as needed.

Step 4 (Resources and sources): With the problem statement pinned down, a second meeting is necessary to define the budget to be invested, plus the human resources and how much of their time will be allocated to this search. Also at this time, the communities to be targeted should be determined. The problem statement, budget, and communities to be targeted can be used to determine which approach to crowdsourcing to adopt: for example, directly to the crowd by internal scouts or

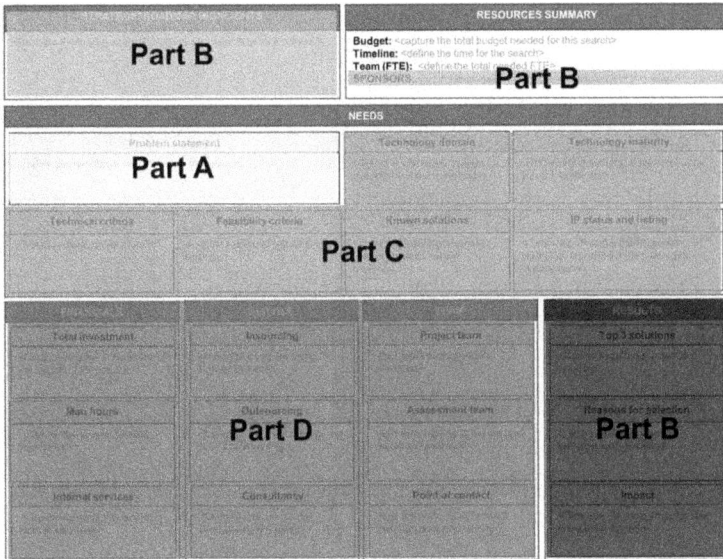

Figure 4.9 Summary of planning process

intrapreneurs[2] or via outsourcing by hiring an intermediary or consultancy firm (part D) and whether to rely solely on the web or to conduct other outreach as well.

The results of these four steps are used to prepare a second draft of the problem statement. It too is circulated through the team and assessed by the tester. As before, the feedback is captured and used to refine the completed form.

Following these four simple steps, sketched in the graphic as shown in Figure 4.9, will guarantee you and your team create a useful and effective problem statement for dissemination. We emphasize crowdsourcing is not cost-free. Resources have to be allocated to preparing for it if the problem statement has to be simple to understand, direct, clear, and effective.

---

[2] An inside entrepreneur, or an entrepreneur within a large firm, who uses entrepreneurial skills without incurring the risks associated with those activities. (www.investopedia.com/terms/i/intrapreneur.asp)

Conducting Outreach in Ways That Keep the Focus of the Crowd

We have just seen that clarity is essential for writing a needs statement. The needs statement communicates to both your in-house team and the external world what your company is looking for.

In order to participate in your contests or challenges, the crowd needs to be clear about what they should look into and think about. The needs statement is necessary but not sufficient for an effective solicitation. The solicitation package should include

- The problem statement;
- The type of solutions sought;
- The IP protection desired for solutions proposed, if any;
- How they will be evaluated;
- What is not sought (which includes any constraints that will eliminate any proposed solutions);
- The confidentiality with which submittals will be treated;
- The type of reward (if any);
- What to include in submittals and how to submit them;
- Any limitations on who can submit or what can be submitted (e.g., no export-controlled technology); and
- A statement that an accepted submittal does not necessarily lead to a contract but may lead to additional discussions if there is interest.

The use of pictures, drawings, or examples when describing a problem can be advantageous, but they have to be well thought out. Graphics and examples can help attract potential contributions, but the visual material could be a double-edged sword since it may be misinterpreted and cause spurious submittals or limit the range of solutions proposed.

A hypothetical example of a challenge solicitation posted by a company in the sport garments and accessories sector is in Table 4.1.

The intrinsic dilemma in outreach is you want to encourage responses, but you do not want to receive useless "junk." Considering the number of participants that could respond to your challenge or contest, the guidance on what to submit is critical. Useful things to request include:

Table 4.1 An example of a challenge

The challenge

Our company is a leading manufacturer in sport garments and accessories. In our shoes division we have faced the problem of eliminating the laces in some agonistic equipment. For our new range of climbing and trekking shoes we want to create a new generation of laces free shoes. We are therefore looking for innovative solutions and/or technologies on how to avoid laces in these products.

The submitted solutions shall be provided in electronic format, and we welcome a full explanation of the idea, accompanied by any kind of informative or supportive material. Sketches, drawings, CAD files, and detailed documentation is definitely a plus.

Solutions:

We do not privilege any specific technological domain, and are open to any solution coming from any individual, team or company that would like to submit their solutions

The level or maturity of the technology shall be in the prototype or in a pre-industrialization phase. The solution shall be easily implementable in our production lines, and ready for ramping up to mass production in a short period of time. We will not discard solutions that should still need development, but they will not be given a priority.

The solution shall be able to undergo some specific tests for ensuring comfort, safety, performance and durability of the shoe. At the same time specific tests will be done in order to ensure comfort, safety, and performance of the athlete.

We look for:
- Flexibility in terms of adaptability to our products
- Compatibility with knitted fabrics
- Flexible and soft enough for ensuring the comfort
- Ergonomic
- Long lasting (at least 5 years)

We are *not* looking for:
- Harmful or unsafe solutions
- Unflexible solutions
- Metallic fabrics
- Thermo shrinking polymers

IP status:
We are interested in hearing solutions already IP protected, as well as not.

Reward:
The winning solution will be awarded with a visit to our development teams and our premise, but more important we will offer a co-development opportunity to the contributor(s).

- Description of the solution, possibly with drawings;
- Technical details clarifying how well it meets the company's advertised decision criteria;
- IP status;
- Who invented the solution and where they were employed at the time;
- Costs to build and to acquire – at least a rough "guesstimate"; and
- Contact details, including the position of the proposer (employed, unemployed, self-employed, etc.).

A quick comment on IP status is warranted. It is an important consideration to clarify whether the idea or the solution can be protected from use by others. A patent filed less than a year ago on a technology not discussed before filing is desirable as it can still be registered in any additional countries of interest to your company.

The reason for asking the position of the proposer is related to the IP status of the solution. Where solvers are employed, their employment contract, the law of the country of the invention, or the law of the country where the inventor lives and works may grant title to all inventions by that individual to the employer. The last thing you want is to get involved in a lawsuit over theft of IP.

Of course, it is not enough to just post your solicitation on your website or some intermediary's portal. Proactive outreach is needed to make people aware that it is out there. No one can monitor everything of interest on the web. For this reason, it is important to post announcements in relevant LinkedIn groups, list servers, and discussion groups of relevant trade associations and professional societies, and send press releases to blogs and the relevant trade and business press. You may also want to send press releases to intermediaries in the technology transfer and commercialization business and to incubators, accelerators, and the like. Basically, you want a description of, and link to, your solicitation to be seen in any channel monitored by relevant communities. When sending out press releases, it is worthwhile considering using a service, such as Business Wire, PR Newswire, Marketwired, or another press release agency. The reason for using one of the services is your press release is more likely to be picked up. But as with any intermediary, there is a fee for the service. Be aware that not all agencies have the same presence in all industrial sectors or geographic regions.

Gathering and Assessing the Solutions

Once the need is defined and before bringing it to the attention of the crowd, you need to have in place mechanisms to collect and evaluate responses. There are two main ways, which are the same ones we saw when describing the top-down approach. One is to use a company website or Dropbox and company staff to conduct the evaluations. The other is to use external intermediaries (or consultancies).

SMEs should consider that the number of solutions that will be proposed is almost impossible to predict. It is affected by the saliency of the problem, the size of the relevant communities, and the outreach conducted. In our experience, solutions often come from many different sources, some of which did not seem obvious prior to getting hit with replies.

Clerical staff can do the basic collection and acknowledgment of submittals. We suggest having a shared drive, folder, or database where the solutions are stored. This repository should have permission-based access, since reviewers will need to enter and view the replies, prepare evaluations, and store those for use by decision makers.

As with preparing the solicitation, it is important to have a formal process for evaluation of the responses. Usually, at least some of the same people who prepared the solicitation are involved in this assessment, as they know what they were looking for. Regardless, it is important to train everyone in both the process for assessment and the metrics to be used to avoid interrater reliability problems.

As soon as the team is formally assigned and proposals start coming in, the team can begin gathering and evaluating the incoming solutions for basic compliance with the rules for submittal. More substantive review should wait, if possible, until after the submission closing date of the challenge or contest. By conducting all the evaluations over one time period, they are more likely to receive the same treatment and it is easier to compare and rank the replies against each other as they are fresher in the team's memory. Of course, in case the challenge is still open, and solutions are submitted, it is possible to start the assessment before the closure, although it is not really cost-effective. In any case, it is beneficial to have a clear stepwise approach in place as well.

Step 1 (Clustering): Cluster the solutions by region of provenience, by technology domains, or by some other relevant criterion. It does not really matter what you use; the important thing is to have them clustered in order to facilitate conducting the assessment in a systematic manner.

Step 2 (List and rank): Catalog the responses in a suitable file format, such as a spreadsheet or database. The clerical staff logging the responses in can initially prepare the catalog. They can place the title of the proposed solution, the abstract, and the proposer, and give each one a unique identifier. The locus of review then shifts to the professionals on the team. Using the title and abstract, they can do a quick first assessment and rank solutions in terms of whether to take them to the next level of evaluation, to park them as potentially interesting if nothing better turns up, or to discard because they are not aligned with the problem statement. Note that at this point who submitted them is not important. The first cut has to be based on whether they solve the problem or challenge that leads to the crowdsourcing initiative. The ones making it through this funnel are put on the list for further review.

Step 3 (Review the top solutions): Once the list has been developed, it is time for the reviewers to read the entire submittals for the solutions on it and to assess them against the previously established metrics. After that has been done, a face-to-face or virtual meeting can be used to discuss and rank order the solutions. At this meeting, a further ranking exercise is usually beneficial. This ranking is based on which of the proposed solutions are easily feasible and implementable, which need further development and thus likely require higher expenditures, and which need more discussion and review to even determine if they are feasible. In other words, they are ranked in terms of likely risk and cost. The outcome of this evaluation is a short list. If the short list emerging from this funnel is not too long, all the ones that are feasible and implementable can be further evaluated. If the new list seems sparse, the ones needing further development or more discussion and review can be added to the short list. If the short list is still too long given available time and resources for the crowdsourcing, an additional down selection based on secondary criteria is appropriate in order to select which replies the team will follow up with.

Sept 4 (Follow up with the contributor): After the final short list is determined, it is time to follow up with the contributors. There are different possibilities on how to do this. Visits can be made to the contributor, the contributors can be invited to the company, or a web conference conducted. (We prefer web to telephone conferences as you can see the contributor's face and often a prototype or something else enhancing the credibility that the solution actually exists or can exist.) Regardless of how it is conducted, the company's review team probes all the solutions on the short list to make a decision on whether to continue exploring acquisition of the solution or not. In the case of continuation, at least in business-driven crowdsourcing, at this point there is usually a shift from nonconfidential discussions to confidential ones held under nondisclosure agreements. The team now assesses both the technical and financial viability of the proposed solution. Questions are asked, demos requested and conducted, and a rough acquisition and adoption plan developed. Also clarified are the economic terms of any deal to acquire the solution. This exploration and discussion should be conducted as transparently and collaboratively as possible, since if a deal moves forward, both parties will have to work together to ensure success. Honest and frank discussions and feedback in both directions are very important as it serves to establish the trust essential for implementing any deal and to maintain the will of the contributors not selected to participate in your crowdsourcing initiatives in the future.

Once the likely winning solution or solutions are identified, a final assessment, sometimes called an impact assessment, should be done. This assessment is to understand whether the solution or solutions are actually feasible to adopt and implement or not. Many companies neglect to do such assessments. There are several reasons why companies do not want to invest their employees' time in such assessment. For example, the utility of the solution may appear obvious, and, thus, further review is seen as a waste of time and money. We stress that this attitude is dangerous, as without an impact assessment, it is difficult to determine the discount rate and all the expenses to apply when doing a net discounted cash flow analysis of the solution prior to making the final decision to go forward and announce a winner. Without such a cash flow analysis, however, there is no way of making a truly educated guess as to whether investments in the product development will have a high or a low probability of financial success.

Impact analysis requires active involvement of internal company experts as well as the contributor of the proposed solution. In them, the company examines the impact that the proposed solution will have on the product, on the product line and family, and on the business. As risks and problems are identified, the contributor is brought in to discuss how these risks and problems can be mitigated or avoided. Depending on the complexity of adopting and implementing a solution, the content of impact assessment is tailored accordingly.

Some common elements apply to any impact assessment. The assessment must examine the impact of the proposed solution on design, manufacturing, sales, customer support, and all the processes captured in Michael Porter's value chain. Earlier, we looked at the adoption and development process for the solution. Here we look at what, if any, impacts that process has on ongoing and future company activities. Where impacts may delay other activities or cause increases in their costs, risks exist. These risks, and how easy it is to avoid or mitigate them, must be added to the discount rate previously used to conduct the cash flow analysis for the solution's adoption, since that previous rate only captured the risks in the immediate adoption and use of the solution. Further, these risks may not all kick in at the same time. So the impact analysis may have to enable the development of discount rates that vary over time.

Step 5 (Rewarding): Once a final selection is made, it should be communicated to the winning contributors and the reward provided in the shortest term possible. As we said previously, this reward could be money, further collaboration, or even a job for the submitter. In any case, the winner, or winners, should be disclosed to the public and to all other contributors in recognition of the good work.

The assessment process is sketched in the next graphic, Figure 4.10.

One suggestion is that the assessing team should be very clear from the beginning on the level of maturity and the ease of implementing the solution. We have seen some companies select very interesting solutions

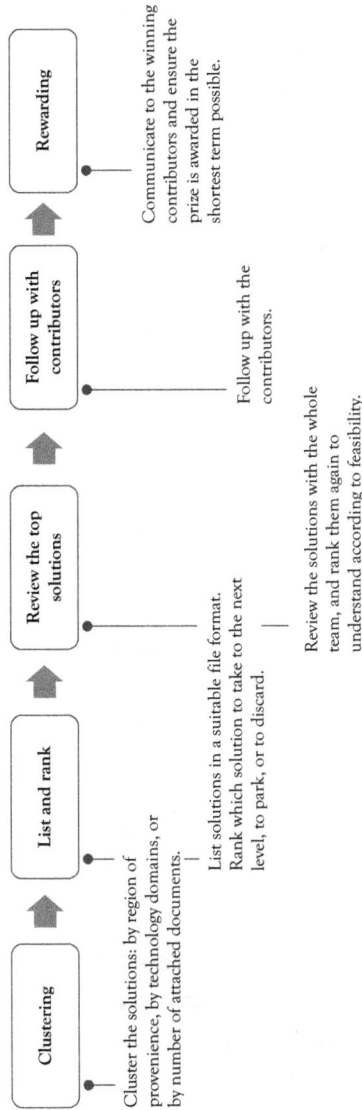

Clustering

Cluster the solutions: by region of provenience, by technology domains, or by number of attached documents.

List and rank

List solutions in a suitable file format. Rank which solution to take to the next level, to park, or to discard.

Review the top solutions

Review the solutions with the whole team, and rank them again to understand according to feasibility.

Follow up with contributors

Follow up with the contributors.

Rewarding

Communicate to the winning contributors and ensure the prize is awarded in the shortest term possible.

Figure 4.10 Assessment process

based on the potential added value to the product. Unfortunately, they rejected using a balanced scorecard that included ease of implementation and integration into the product. In these cases, we have noticed that the company struggled quite a lot in further development of the technology, since it was not that easy to implement, and thus the burn rate during product development destroyed the anticipated value add since too much money was spent getting to market to enable hitting the anticipated return on investment.

Assessing the Feasibility

Even after a solution is selected, it may not be useable. A feasibility study is useful for understanding if the solution is indeed feasible, reproducible, and industrially scalable. Usually as part of this assessment, a prototype is made in order to physically determine whether the solution adapts and embeds correctly and then works as expected. The making of a prototype could be also important for the so-called alpha testing, since it could be used to check several different preset parameters to verify if the product is working according to the one as originally designed. Sometimes the solution's adaptation and embedment is modeled in software during the alpha phase and then physically implemented in order to enable beta testing by likely lead customers.

Once the feasibility of the solution is checked and validated, it is time to enter the real product development phase, which will basically bring the product to the market in a definite time lapse.

Choosing Intermediaries

Intermediaries have proliferated ever since people started licensing and selling inventions. In a very interesting survey, Diener and Piller defined a class of intermediaries called Open Innovation Accelerators (OIAs).[3] In their survey, they analyze the different kinds of intermediaries

---

[3] Diener, K., and F. Piller. May 2013. *The Market for Open Innovation: The 2013 RWTH Open Innovation Accelerator Survey*. 2nd ed. Raleigh, NC: Lulu Publishing.

offering services to companies that are now part of the ecosystem of innovation. We do not discuss here intermediaries offering software, tools for innovation, or intellectual asset and IP management, since they are not in the scope of this chapter. We do, however, discuss how to determine if an intermediary offering crowdsourcing services is worth hiring.

Network

In our experience, what is most important for a crowdsourcing intermediary is the network of solution providers. The network of solution providers is usually a self-developing entity. The more interesting the challenges posed by the intermediary and the better the rewards offered, the more likely the intermediary will attract solution providers to its network. These networks are like the tip of an iceberg. Those in the networks, in turn, work and collaborate with others, which means word of mouth de facto extends the network beyond those formally registered as part of it. The members of the network often connect via other channels to other people who can provide part or all of the solutions being sought. Some of the people in the extended "hidden" network team up the registered members to submit solutions. Of course, the best networks and extensions consist of people with the right experience, education, and creativity to provide plausible solutions with high regularity.

For an SME interested in conducting crowdsourcing through an intermediary, the first question has to be, who participates in the intermediary's network? That determines if the likely inflow of contributions will be good or poor. Asking a few simple questions helps determine if the intermediary is worth retaining.

- How big is the network: the real and the virtual? (The real one is the one that the intermediary effectively reaches, and the virtual is the one it claims to potentially reach by word of mouth).
- Which types of challenges, or contests, are posted on the portal? (Specific technology domains, various, scientific, engineering, ideas, etc.)

- What is the success rate of the challenges and contests in general and in areas closely related to your problem? (Are they matched, are there any winners, and how many? These are all questions that will indicate to you the real level of contribution.)
- What are the average profiles of contributors? (PhDs, graduates, common people, inventors, consultants, etc.)

Support and Services

Another aspect to probe when considering retaining an intermediary is the support and services offered. Some intermediaries simply provide a portal where you can post challenges. Others help companies to define their needs, develop their solicitation documents, conduct outreach, and collect and evaluate the replies. They may do these tasks as contract labor or they may train employees of the SME in how to do these for themselves. Coaching and mentoring may be offered alongside the training.

Some intermediaries also offer additional related services such as portal creation and maintenance. Intermediaries may own these portals or they may create one specifically for your company. Such portals are usually a one-way submission platforms. A person or company can submit ideas and solutions responding to a specific challenge or contest. These submissions are then reviewed by the intermediary for compliance or forwarded directly to the company placing the solicitation. Where the intermediary owns portals, a fee is charged for use and support activities.

Another set of services are provided "offline" as synchronous "live" activities. Examples include cocreation sessions, hackathons, lead user contests, or any similar activity that aims at bringing "crowdsourced" professionals together to work on a common challenge or contest. Such real-time live services are important where a solution is needed right away.

Of course, the more support or services used, the higher the price charged by the intermediary. That makes service modules attractive as you only need to buy what you need. The quality of service usually also will affect the fees charged.

As when hiring any vendor, an SME should approach an intermediary with a clear understanding of what it wants to get out of an engagement and what it can afford to pay. The SME should negotiate the price rather than take whatever is offered. In many cases, intermediaries offer discounts depending on how much is bought, whether the SME is a repeat customer, whether business is slow for the intermediary, and the like.

Solutions

The only reason to use an intermediary is that is likely to get you better solutions less expensively than you could yourself. Sometimes what makes a solution more affordable is that the intermediary will do the work on commission (on a success fee) or a combination of a modest up-front fee or retainer plus a commission on your adoption of the solution.

There are a myriad of alternatives found in market. Some intermediaries offer co-ownership of solutions under which the patent remains with the current IP owner, and the SME conducting open innovation receives a license restricted to specific fields of use, geographic regions, time frames, and so on. Some intermediaries may even coinvest in acquiring or implementing the solution in exchange for a piece of the downstream revenues from product sales. Others may already own portfolios of IP that they have bundled together in anticipation of market needs. Such bundling is more common in industries like biotech and information technology, where patent stacking occurs. Patent stacking means multiple patents are licensed and "stacked" on top of each other in order to assemble the IP portfolio needed to make a product without infringing the rights of others. The intermediary makes money by bundling the stacks and then offering nonexclusive licenses to the bundle. Buying a bundle reduces IP transaction costs for companies seeking licenses, enabling them to make and sell products.

Again, it is essential that your company approaches an intermediary as you would any other vendor. Be very clear about what you are looking for and what you are willing to pay to get it. Then you can compare intermediaries based on their offerings, track records, and customer references.

Profiling the Crowd to Source

When using crowdsourcing, as said previously, it is important to be clear on the community to approach and the type of individuals that a company is aiming to involve in the activities. Defining the "profile" for your primary target is essential, because it is clear that how you approach a community of engineers will be different from how you approach a community of chefs. Although crowdsourcing is based on the premise that solutions can come from anywhere, and nonobvious solutions may come from unobvious sources, it still helps to develop a profile for your ideal contributors. We tend to think about contributor profiles in three ways—by industry or economic sector, by profession or occupation, and by role. Roles are archetypes in open innovation. Some typical profiles in crowdsourcing are shown in Figure 4.11.

As Figure 4.11 makes clear, roles in crowdsourcing are defined in terms of their proactiveness or reactiveness to a company's needs. In targeting roles, the emphasis should be on reaching those profiles that are willing and able to provide solutions.

Doers are the people a company should definitely target. These are the people who want to solve the problems posed and will engage in the challenge or contest. Doers are mainly professionals, such as inventors

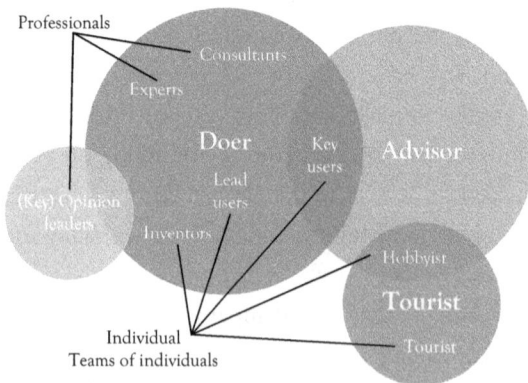

Figure 4.11 Types of crowds. Crowds have many faces. To choose which contributor to address, it is important to be clear on the needs and the type of contribution sought

and experts, lead users, and, in some cases, consultants. The people filling this role are driven by many different motivations, but they are the active contributors of solutions.

Inventors are usually persons who like to create something new that is outside the box of convention. Inventors are visionaries. They are extremely creative persons with excellent technical skills. As out-of-the-box thinkers, they exhibit a special knack or instinct for seeing solutions to problems. In many cases, this knack makes them seem to be very eclectic professionals. Inventors are usually innovators as well, as they want to see their inventions deployed for practical purposes.

This archetype is very much sought after in crowdsourcing because they are real problem solvers. They actively seek to provide solutions to whatever need is present. These proactive individuals enjoy participating in ideas and crowdsourcing portals both for the enjoyment of invention and for the monetary rewards and honor it can bring. Inventors and lead users are the critical roles to target if you want to succeed at crowdsourcing new products and technologies.

Experts are people who have a specific field of expertise, usually gained through education and life or professional experience in a specific domain. There is a body of research that suggests experts are better at short-term predictions and incremental innovation as they become captives of their own expertise—which acts as blinders to seeing unconventional solution paths. They can be found via intermediaries, through companies providing connections to experts, or simply by scanning the names commonly appearing as presenters and keynoters of relevant meetings and conferences, by doing citation analysis of scholarly journals and the trade press to see who often publishes and who is often cited, and by contacting the committee chairs at trade associations and professional societies. They are useful as commentators on crowdsourcing portals, but where experts really shine is in one-to-one discussions and activities. Retaining experts can be expensive, but by being able to quickly put their finger on the solution to a problem, what they cost per hour is offset by the shorter time it takes to reach a solution. They are particularly useful when they provide expertise that is lacking in a company and insights that never occurred to a project team.

Lead users[4] perform a role that has been studied extensively by academics. They are sometimes called innovators following the practice of Everett Rogers in his seminal book *Diffusion of Innovations*. They are the first to adopt a new technology and have a combination of technical and inventive skills. They are different from inventors, since their focus is on bringing the inventions of others into practical use. They are demanding, but simply because they want the next greatest thing.

Rogers studied innovation adoption across a number of fields. He found that around 2.5 percent of the total addressable market of users[5] would adopt a new product before it is established in the market. (See the darker curve in Figure 4.12.) They are tinkerers, practitioners of what used to be called Yankee ingenuity, making them both proactive and reactive at the same time. They may proactively improve a specific product or service or they may reactively wait until a company introduces some new "gadget" or "toy" that they can play with.

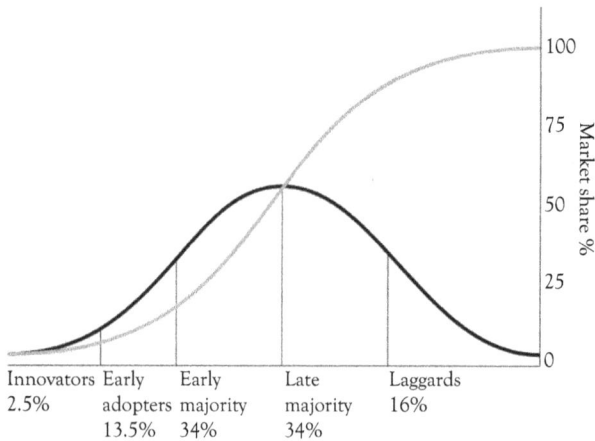

Figure 4.12 The innovation cycle

Source: Wikipedia, http://commons.wikimedia.org/wiki/File:Diffusion_of_ideas.svg

---

[4] Von Hippel, E. 1986. "Lead Users: A Source of Novel Product Concepts." *Management Science* 32, no. 7, pp. 791–806.
[5] Rogers, E.M. 1962. *Diffusion of Innovations*. Glencoe: Free Press. ISBN 0-612-62843-4

Companies benefit when lead users frequent their crowdsourcing portal. In addition to providing solutions themselves, they often are catalysts on the portal or when attending cocreation workshops or ideation events. They encourage others to invent what they cannot themselves.

Consultants are mainly active as professionals who create a link between the company posting a need and a potential solver. The role of consultants is clearly defined, but they are not always taken into account in the proposal of solutions, because they are seen as another intermediary. A consultant is usually also an expert, but this depends really on the type of tasks required of them. Essentially, consultants are outsourced staff who, by working for a number of different entities, gather a bag of best practices and tricks of the trade to offer to their customers. In crowdsourcing, they often function as facilitators and catalysts.

Opinion leaders, as the name implies, are the people others turn to for advice. They are part of Rogers's early adopters group in Figure 4.12. There are many studies on who they usually are and how central this profile is for successful product innovation. Opinion leaders influence others because they are respected. Because of their stature in a community, even though they only occasionally propose solutions to crowdsource problems, their interest in a problem can drive certain discussions, inventions, and innovations by others.

Companies will definitely involve them in crowdsourcing, as they are nodal points in communication channels relying on word of mouth. As such, they are great resources for outreach and bringing the voice of the customer into open innovation. A smart company provides them with new products to review and comment on. Their critiques and suggestions for improvement can make or break a product launch, since others will defer to their judgment about a new product.

Advisors consist of key users and hobbyists. They provide perspective, insights, and a sounding board for companies engaged in crowdsourcing. When advisors are hired to give advice, they become experts or consultants. In those roles, the financial business relationship skews the impartiality of the insights being offered, making it qualitatively different than advice.

Key users are just that, the intended customers for the results of open innovation once they have been productized and brought to market.

As advisors, they are the oft-sought "voice of the customer." They are common users of specific kinds of products or services relevant for the problem statement. We like to distinguish them from lead users on the basis of being proactive consumers. They are the more vocal members of one of the customer segments of the company. Usually they become key users when they have been disappointed by a company's product, when a product has some missing features, or when the product is not providing the functionality they were looking for. In the most of cases, they are complainants, but they are also proactive enough to care about the brand they use, or choose, and for this reason, they turn to be real advisors. It is rare to see them participating in challenges or contests, but they sometimes step into doer behavior and then try to solve a problem by becoming lead users. Most of the time, however, they are visiting crowdsourcing portals to ask for a new product or a new product feature or functionality without necessarily thinking about how to develop that product, feature, or functionality. They make good targets for market research activities like focus groups or product testing.

Hobbyists are people with relevant technical capabilities who, for whatever reason, do not want to or are not capable of submitting their own complete solutions. They are helpful for proposing improvements on other solutions and for suggesting solution pathways. What they do not provide is actual complete solutions due to time constraints, limited relevant technical capabilities, contractual obligations to others, and the like.

A hobbyist is in a role that has aspects of the tourist and the advisory. Usually a hobbyist is a person who has interests that intersect with the needs posted by the soliciting company. As the name implies, hobbyists are on the portal because of an avocation rather than a vocation. Accordingly, they may propose a solution if it pops into their head. They are unlikely to "work" at it in order to win the reward. They may also comment on solutions or help other solvers by suggesting potential improvements to the solutions of others. They are "latent" contributors, by which we mean they have the full potential and capability to propose solutions to the problem statement. They just do not have an economic motivation that drives them to work at it. Despite their low contribution level, they are good sources of insights and advice. They contribute a brainstorming perspective and suggestions that can trigger solutions by others.

Tourists are individuals who are mainly curious (*tourists* indeed). Tourists are persons who like to be informed about the challenges and contests that are posted. They are usually not active in presenting solutions and are minimally involved in the discussions. They tend to surf through the portals or visit the platforms where companies place their posts and have a look at what is going on. Their aim is, in most cases, simply to be informed, in order to have a quick overview of the needs of companies. Tourists may be employees of competitors, journalists, consultants, (trend or business) analysts, or professionals trolling for work. Although curious and attracted by the possibility of contributing, more often than not, tourists leave "useless" comments on the portal.

Most tourists are just curious about the state of the art in a field and enjoy seeing creative minds at work. The category also includes hobbyists who are there to gather new ideas for their own purposes and have little interest in submitting solutions to the posted solicitation. Sometimes, tourists have more sinister motivations. They may be checking in and reviewing crowdsourcing solicitations as a way of conducting competitive intelligence on companies.

Tourists are not useful to a company seeking to solve a problem today, but they could be useful in the future if a future challenge or contest triggers them to develop a solution. Monitoring tourists can be useful for "counterintelligence" on competitors. The posting company can also mine tourists to find participants for focus groups, advisers, new customers, and the like.

Tourists are always a way to stimulate word of mouth about a crowdsourcing initiative. Indeed, since they usually try to be informed, they are also very willing to share what they have seen with others. They may discuss a solicitation on social media, tell colleagues or friends, or write about a solicitation in their blog.

Motivations and Rewards

Working with a crowd requires taking into account many different behavioral aspects. Here we focus on the expectations of the crowd in terms of rewards. Paraphrasing George Bernard Shaw: "If you have an idea and I have an idea and we exchange these ideas, then each of us will have two ideas." To get ideas, crowdsourcing relies on the levers of motivation and rewards.

For companies interested in repeatedly using crowdsourcing, it is vital to remember that sourcing from the crowd has a price. Just what a fair price is depends on what others are offering for crowdsourced solutions and what potential contributors will see as a fair exchange for their ideas, concepts, designs, technology, and solutions in general. Depending on the type of contributor that a company wants to involve, the motivating prize will vary.

In general, recognition is the best reward, because many solvers are willing to share their ideas simply to have the recognition and honor that comes when the idea is acknowledged as an important innovation worthy of being launched in the market. Of course, recognition motivates even better when it is accompanied by significant financial rewards. People like to be rewarded with monetary prizes. After all, since the company posting the crowdsourcing solicitation is going to use it to make money, it seems fair that the person or people who contributed the idea should get a piece of the action.

The prize money should be set to be significant but not too high. Think in terms of orders of magnitude and hop one or more orders higher than the anticipated contributors normally see. For a person whose hourly wage is $10, $100 or $1,000 is a lot of money. For a person who earns $10,000 a week, $100 is pocket change and $1,000 is real money but not a lot of it.

In general, people feel that what is fair to pay for an idea is also tied to how much money the idea could make and how wealthy the buyer is. Solution providers often suspect that behind an anonymous challenge on an intermediary's portal is a big company that can afford to spend money to get the right idea to solve its problem. We also have learned that in some cases, contrary to what seems intuitive, people tend to be scared away by very high prizes because they believe "this is out of my capabilities." For instance, in cases where students are targeted, if the prize is too high, participation is typically lower because the students are discouraged by their own perception that the challenge requires very skilled professionals to solve it.

While important, money and recognition are not the only useful motivations. Also important is the chance to make a difference. Many people do not just want to provide an idea or a technology; they also want to be instrumental in bringing their innovation into use by participating as a codeveloper of the new product.

For companies, entering a supply chain brings financial and reputational benefits and personal satisfaction for those involved. Potential new suppliers can work hard to provide a very thorough solution, with a detailed idea, drawings, and a working prototype as a proof of their concept and the value of bringing them into a firm's supply chain.

Offering some resources for developing the submitted solution is a way for companies to attract talents from the crowd and to engage with them. Some companies would really like to help the solver and provide a means for implementing the solution. They could make available some budget, expert personnel for supporting, laboratories, and any other means that could help in creating a fully functioning product. In some cases, those talents are hired, and in this way, they could be fully involved in the project for developing their own idea.

Last but not least, a company could also reward a contributor with shares (or royalties) on the income they earn after the product has been launched on the market. This case is being discussed last because it is typical of those collaborations that ask for the provision of specific creative inputs such as idea contests and design contests. For completeness, we include equity and royalties, even though they are less common in "crowdsolving."

Whatever the type of reward the company is willing to offer, we would like to stress once again that it is important they determine it based on the type of crowd being targeted. Different types of crowds are driven by different motivations, and therefore, they will engage in the challenge, or contest, with different behaviors depending on how interested they are and the rewards being offered. Recognition, monetary prizes, collaboration, and business opportunities are all motivational aspects that have to be considered well in advance, when needs are discussed and the challenge or contest solicitation drafted.

A company should also be attentive in linking the motivation and reward to the complexity of the challenge or contest. It is clear that if the request is very complex and the solution sought is indeed quite challenging, the reward shall be set accordingly. In some cases, solvers do not participate in a challenge because they think the need is complex and the reward is too low.

At the same time, another aspect to take into account is transparency. Increasingly nowadays, the name of the company conducting crowdsourcing is being revealed so that a solver knows which company she or he is providing a solution to. This aspect is also very important because it sets financial expectations as well as sends a message to the crowd that the company is really open and ready for new innovations. Of course, the practice of open innovation needs to be guided by the strategies of the company.

IP Protection

IP is a very sensitive subject whenever a challenge or a contest is posted for crowdsourcing. Many companies, especially the big corporations, have very strict terms and conditions, and in most cases, they ask to retain any IP that might result from implementing a submission. How important IP protection is for SMEs depends on the nature of the product and the market it will enter. IP is less important where products have very short life cycles, such as in software apps. There, first mover advantage may affect market success far more than IP protection. What is needed is freedom to operate rather than freedom to exclude others.

One of the most common mistakes of SMEs is to not think thoroughly about IP protection. We have seen many SMEs without protection or a strong nondisclosure agreement in place beforehand. This is wrong because IP generation and protection can be a value enhancer on both the income statement and the balance sheet of both solicitor and solver.

As a general rule, where solutions are being transferred as part of crowdsourcing, there is at least the trade secret involved. Trade secrets protect the know-how developed with respect to how to use a technology. Depending on what the solution is, patent, copyright, or mask may also be involved. Unless there is an explicit transfer of IP rights, each party will retain the IP it created before collaboration. IP created during collaboration will be jointly owned. Knowing what kind of IP protection to seek and how to protect your intellectual assets from leakage is a constant challenge when practicing open innovation.

Smart companies will use everyday language in the terms and conditions that must be agreed to before access to the portal is granted. These terms should appear in an end user license agreement (EULA), which must be agreed to before accesses to the portal is granted. The EULA should include a statement in big black letters that declares that whatever is submitted via the portal will be property of the company. Alternatively, it can state that a royalty-free license to use in any field of use of interest to the company is granted. Such statements can discourage solution submittals. A fallback is to state that the IP stays with the person who files the idea or solution, but the company has a first right of refusal to negotiate a license if the submittal is selected.

Risks of Crowdsourcing

As a conclusion to this chapter, we tackle those less beneficial aspects of crowdsourcing. Everything has its own drawbacks and crowdsourcing is no exception.

Tell the World

Telling the world what you are looking for, for some companies, may not be beneficial. To mitigate this risk, a company can use an intermediary and stay anonymous.

Trust

Presently, many companies are revealing their identity, even when using intermediaries. Contributors relate this shift to the need to build trust between the company and open innovation contributors in order to promote the sharing of innovations. It also enhances the company's goodwill as a firm interested in innovation. Indeed, in a manner analogous to the naming of sports stadiums, companies can use "branding" their challenges to build their own brand's value. Transparency increases the chances of becoming "the partner of choice" for outside inventors and innovators.

Where is the risk then? It is in the fact that building trust is a long process, and it takes very little to break down. Trust is a double-edged sword in the sense that it restricts the behaviors a company can use to compete. Actions that destroy trust have larger adverse consequences for firms focused on building trust than others.

Quantity Versus Quality

Quantity versus quality is another aspect that sometimes is not taken properly into account. Unless well planned and executed, a company can be overwhelmed by the number of responses to a crowdsourcing initiative. Large volumes of responses mean higher costs to separate the wheat from the chaff. On the other hand, poorly designed initiatives can result in too few responses to generate anything useful. That also means a waste of money. A successful challenge or contest requires a well-thought-out solicitation and a well-executed outreach plan.

The quality issue is sometimes seen where companies use social media to promote their crowdsourcing initiative. If the social media outreach goes viral, the company can be deluged with potential solutions from around the world. A careful evaluation of the utility of social media in outreach is required, especially where the solution being sought is likely complex and requires a specific set of expertise and capabilities to pull off.

Binding Terms and Conditions

Working with crowds requires being flexible enough to negotiate in order to acquire the best possible solution. Yet if the context or challenge rules require certain things, such as royalty-free right to use the winning submission, it may be hard to acquire the best technology. Its owners may insist on negotiating changes to the terms and conditions found in the crowdsourcing solicitation. Unfortunately, changing the terms and conditions to accommodate the winner can lead to cries of foul play. Yet if that is not done, an opportunity may be lost. Alternatively, the terms and conditions can be so restrictive that no one wants to float a solution.

The entire initiative can be derailed if your company is perceived to be pandering.

Cultural Differences

Last but not least, there is the risk involved in cultural differences. Usually reaching a vast crowd spread across a myriad of different locations will involve also managing cultural differences. Different cultures approach challenges and contests in different ways. The cultural variations need not be driven by nationality. The pace of work is different in small rural communities than in large metropolitans. Words that mean one thing in one language can be mistranslated and end up meaning something else.

Takeaways

Crowdsolving is a way for SMEs to access a number of solutions to their problems. By posting a challenge or creating a contest, a company having, or facing, a product, manufacturing, or other issues can hold a contest and use the best submittal. Almost always, this approach is less expensive than if the solution is developed in-house. But crowdsourcing almost always requires a well-planned and executed initiative. It is an intriguing dance of seemingly infinite possibilities.

There are four key takeaways from this chapter we want to highlight:

1. <u>Be clear on your needs</u>: a company should be very clear on their needs and be able to write them in a consistent and understandable way. Using the right language to address the right crowd is essential for avoiding bad surprises and for getting solutions going straight to the core of the problem. Writing a need proposal is a kind of art and is a continuous learning; the more precise the proposal, the clearer the problem to be solved is to the company and to the crowd. Guidelines have been provided, but practice is the key for improving the way a company describes their needs, the metrics that will be used to assess submittals, and the constraints that limit what can be a successful solution.

2. <u>Choose the right crowd</u>: the "crowd" has many different faces, since different individuals participate with different levels of involvement and move in and out of the crowd in accordance with their own interests, expertise, experience, health, and knowledge. Crowds change constantly and to keep the focus of those individuals is a must for successful crowdsourcing. Identifying which of the crowds are mostly relevant for a company's search is a matter of the strategic approach to crowdsourcing but is also related to what a company is asking for. Each challenge or contest attracts different types of contributors, with their behavior fostered by specific motivation(s).

3. <u>Structure your approach</u>: a widely defined structure is the starting point for approaching any crowd and sourcing acceptable solutions from there. Step by step, your approach should guide the practitioners of this problem-solving methodology in running an effective campaign. At the heart of this structure is risk mitigation and elimination.

4. <u>Pencil it</u>: when it comes to solving problems, a company always has two choices, make them or buy them. Crowdsourcing is a variant of buying them. Making it pencil requires developing a rough baseline depicting the cost of internally developing a solution. If the right people or capacities are not in-house, this baseline has to include hiring new staff and buying new production machinery, test facilities, and the like. This baseline is compared with the costs of a crowdsourcing campaign. The argument in this chapter is that crowdsourcing can cost less. It is also useful to estimate revenues to see if crowdsourcing pencils. There is some product opportunity or problem driving the product development of which crowdsourcing is a part. The quicker the product development can be completed, the sooner revenues can be generated. Of course, there are risks associated with both revenues and expenses. If the risks can be identified and quantified, we can use discounted cash flow analysis to compare internal development with crowdsourcing. Of course, the key risk in both approaches is that no viable new product or process will be found.

Crowdsourcing is most attractive where disruptive or radical new solutions are being sought. Incremental innovations require a thorough understanding of the current product and its manufacturing method. Next generation products and those of the generation after are less well defined and there is time to bring in and adopt new, "out-of-the-box" solutions.

The way crowdsourcing plays out on an SME's income statement is seen in the costs of goods sold. With crowdsourcing, these go down so long as the cost of labor to evaluate the submittals plus any product development required is less than the cost of an all-internal development effort. Where the internal folks are stumped about what to do next, crowdsourcing also has a big impact on the revenue side—so long as a solution does emerge.

The really challenging part is to figure out the discount rate to use when calculating the net discounted cash flow for the two methods. The trick here is to use the impact analysis to ground your suspicions. Risk is simply a function of delay in getting a product to market or of the necessity of spending additional money beyond what was anticipated. Assuming the time to market is shorter and the cost of R&D and product development is the same, crowdsourcing wins so long as the same discount rate is applied to both.

On the balance sheet, the calculations are even easier. Any new technology acquired is an asset. Similarly, the greater the positive buzz on the crowdsourcing campaign, the greater the rise in goodwill as well as IP intangible assets.

Of course, if nothing is found through crowdsourcing, all intangible asset accounts might nosedive in the light of dwindling gross revenues. The process becomes a loss on the income statement and a reduction of retained earnings on the balance sheet. The discount rate goes up. It is a mess. That is why planning and focus are so important. When crowdsourcing works, it can give a company a big bump. When it fails, there simply is no return on the investment required to do it.

CHAPTER 5

Emergence of the SME as a Source of Market-Ready Technologies

Daniel Satinsky, JD, MALD

Introduction

In the evolving open innovation technology market, savvy entrepreneurs are using an emerging model for developing new technologies that is particularly suited to small and medium enterprises (SMEs). Every entrepreneur knows something about using a start-up or spinout vehicle for realizing his or her dreams of technological and financial success. However, those dreams meet unexpected obstacles with very long business development timelines. In this chapter, we introduce another type of SME, the "spin-up," as an alternative and quicker route to market.

The specific purpose of the spin-up SME is to capitalize on the opportunity created by the confluence of open innovation and the growing number of early-stage technologies. Spin-ups are SMEs formed with the specific purpose of being acquired or of disposing of the technology under development. They are not intended to become fully functioning companies in their market segment. Under the right circumstances, a spin-up can be a much better vehicle for successful technology commercialization than its better-known cousins, the spinout and the start-up.

The keys to success for a spin-up include the ability to identify an early-stage technology that could find market demand, a team combining entrepreneurial and technical skills, intellectual property (IP) that can be protected and later marketed, market intelligence to adapt the technology to market requirements, funding from available grant and

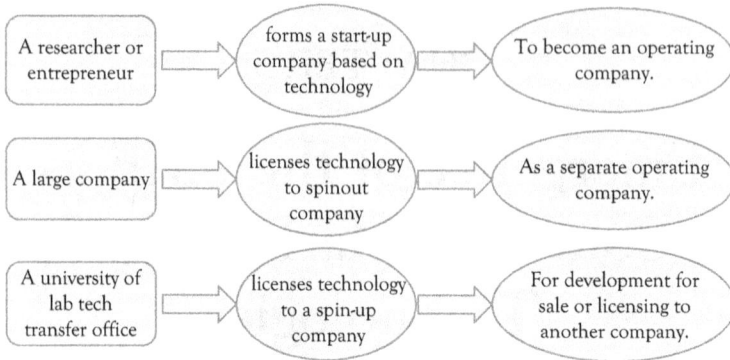

Figure 5.1 Start-ups, spinouts, and spin-ups

Abbreviation: TRL, technology readiness level.

investment capital sufficient to finance the development cycle, and an exit strategy aligned with the overall model. Taken together, this model can be described as a spin-up model.

The fundamental institutional forces that lead to the creation of spinouts, start-ups, and spin-ups, as shown in Figure 5.1, are the same. All are part of the growing trend for an SME to become a source for market-ready technologies. The differences between these different types of SMEs have to do with the different functional purposes for which each is formed. For our purposes, the common basis for all three is the existence of a new technology that appears to have the potential for profitable use in the market. The difference has to do with the ultimate intentions of the founders for each type of SME.

Start-ups and spinouts are founded with the goal of becoming fully functioning companies selling products or services. There is much written about start-ups and spinouts, almost with a mythology of their own. However, from our examination of market trends, we believe that there is an opportunity for spin-up companies in sectors not related to biotech, social networking, gaming, or Internet marketing and service delivery. There is an important gap in the open innovation environment for spin-up companies in providing market-ready, innovative technologies for the more traditional industrial and service sectors that are also undergoing continuous growth and technological change.

Our use of the term spin-up as outlined in this chapter is unique and different in its goals from those of a spinout or start-up. We have conceptualized a spin-up as a model in which promising early-stage technologies are moved up the technology readiness level (TRL) to increase their ultimate value as component parts in a supply chain or as part of a product line. The goal of a spin-up SME from the beginning is to bring the technology into the open innovation market for acquisition by others, either through licensing or through acquisition of the spin-up company.

The business model for a spin-up company rests on a quicker route to market than a spinout or a start-up. The financial model for the spin-up company is based on monetization of the spun-up, developed technology, minus costs for the initial technology licensing, company formation, operations, and development.

Formation of a Spin-Up Company

The basic roadmap for a successful spin-up SME can be summarized as follows:

1. Select a technology that has been evaluated to have commercial potential.
2. Identify the tasks necessary to move the technology to a commercially viable level of technology readiness, expressed as a technology development plan.
3. Create a new legal entity (Newco) to hold the IP rights in the technology and to develop it to a commercially viable TRL.
4. Identify and recruit the development team, including at least a lead principal investigator (PI) and a business manager for Newco.
5. Apportion the equity in Newco to reflect the interests of the inventor, the PI or business manager, and others who are critical for the technology and subsequent successful operations of Newco.
6. Negotiate and close on an option to license the technology to Newco, a no-cost option if possible.
7. Identify the lab or prototyping facility for implementing the development plan.

8. Identify the source of funding for the spin-up company activities and closing the financing for project activities. Depending upon the funding source, a reapportionment of equity may be necessary at this time.

9. Begin executing the technology development plan to raise the TRL of the technology.

10. Exercise the technology license option if the development appears likely to succeed and take a full technology.

11. Market the upgraded technology to a potential licensor or acquirer.

12. Negotiate and close a license deal, including payment of any deferred license or patent fees or sell the company in total.

13. Distribute proceeds or put in place plan for distribution of annual royalties.

The main success factors for practical implementation of this model are technology, team, IP, funding, and an exit plan. All of these factors are described in more detail in the chapter.

Open Innovation Market Opportunity for the Spin-Up Model

As indicated in the introduction to this book, multinational and large companies increasingly look for "outside-in" innovation. This outside-in perspective is that of the large company. The flip side of this formulation is the perspective of the SME that supplies the innovation to be taken in by the multinationals and large companies. In this chapter, we examine the process of absorption of an innovative technology from the point of view of the entrepreneurs and inventors who are forming SMEs to feed this process.

The specific area of opportunity for spin-up SMEs lies in taking technologies that have come out of labs and exist as prototypes but are not mature enough on their own to enter the innovation funnel. These technologies need to be moved up the TRL and adapted to industry specifications before they can be monetized. However, technology development is a complex process that involves sophisticated practical science and engineering combined with business and commercial expertise.

The purpose of a spin-up SME is to bring about this combination that is then capable of taking advantage of the growing open innovation market demand for innovation. The spin-up company is the vehicle to implement a process that bridges the gap between technologies and markets and makes money in the process.

The historic roots of open innovation lie in the breakdown in the connection between industrial research and commercialization. The predominant model for innovation up until the early 1980s was based on sourcing new technology through internal company research and development labs. This began to change as companies like Cisco (founded in 1984) used an open innovation model to outcompete AT&T's Bell Labs, which was at that time the world's largest R&D center.[1] Recent research has shown an ongoing decline in corporate research from 1980 to 2007, demonstrating an ongoing corporate interest in acquiring innovative technology but declining interest in maintaining internal scientific capabilities.[2] This and similar developments let to the paradigm shift in innovation management that is captured in Henry Chesborough's work on open innovation.

This new approach toward sourcing of technology occurred simultaneously with another paradigm shift in the 1980s as the result of passage in 1984 of the U.S. Bayh-Dole Act as the legal framework for the commercialization of government-financed technologies. This Act initiated the expansion of sources of new technologies, as universities, government labs, and private independent research organizations were mandated to put scientific discoveries into practical commercial use.

Increasingly, the mission of many research institutions includes commercialization of their new scientific discoveries and inventions. The results of scientific experimentation can be new inventions but can also be any unique tools developed to manipulate and measure what

---

[1] Gassman, O., B. Widenmayer, S. Friesike, and T. Schildhauer. October 25, 2011. "Opening Up Science: Towards an Agenda of Open Science in Industry and Academia." HIIG Discussion Paper Series. http://ssrn.com/abstract=2091122

[2] Arora, A., S. Belenzon, and A. Patacconi. January 2015. "Killing the Golden Goose? The Decline of Science in Corporate R&D." National Bureau of Economic Research, Working Paper 20902. www.nber.org/papers/w20902

might also qualify as inventions. The commercialization of these inventions is usually technology driven, not market driven. The pool of IP and early-stage technologies is growing dramatically but is most often driven by science-oriented inventors. These new technologies are rarely developed in response to recognized industry demands. When the new technologies enter the market, they are nails looking for hammers. Therefore, an important part of the success of a spin-up company will depend upon the leadership team's skill in identifying companies looking to acquire technologies and tying technology development to the requirements of these companies.

The utility of SMEs as a source of market-ready technologies is a relatively new phenomenon. The importance of this opportunity has been obscured by the common focus on start-ups or spinouts as the potential next Google or Facebook. As transformative as these Internet-related applications have been, they are actually quite rare. They are so rare in fact that they are sometimes referred to as "unicorns," a term used to describe those rare start-ups that achieve billion-dollar valuations. While these success stories drive a lot of media coverage and start-up entrepreneurs, the occurrence of such a company is almost as rare as a unicorn. Venture capitalist Aileen Lee has calculated that as of November 2013, only 1 in every 1,538 startups or 0.7 percent founded in the past decade can be classified as unicorns. For those rare animals to appear as either initial public offerings (IPOs) or acquisitions took an average of seven years.[3] The spin-up model is an alternative for entrepreneurs to reduce the time to market with more realistic assumptions for revenue returns. It is a model with a higher potential success rate and an alternative particularly for entrepreneurs and research scientists who expect to engage in serial commercialization activities.

As noted earlier, the key variables for the success of a spin-up are the team, IP, market intelligence, funding, and an appropriate exit

---

[3] Dempwolf, C.S., J. Auer, and M. D'Ippolito. 2014. "Innovation Accelerators: Defining Characteristics Among Startup Assistance Organizations." Optimal Solutions Group, LLC, quoted in U.S. Small Business Administration website. www.sba.gov/advocacy/innovation-accelerators-defining-characteristics-among-startup-assistance-organizations (accessed November 17, 2014).

plan. Keeping these factors in mind, SMEs interested in being spin-up companies (or entrepreneurs interested in forming them) will need a disciplined and structured approach, such as the one outlined in this chapter to maximize their chances for success.

Technology

There is a lot of technology available for development. According to the Association of University Technology Managers (AUTM) website, prior to 1980, the U.S. federal government held title to 28,000 patents, but fewer than 5 percent were licensed to private industry. After the passage of Bayh-Dole in the United States in 1980, American universities spun off more than 4,000 new companies and licensed many technologies.[4]

The process of transitioning university inventions into innovative technologies is not a simple, straightforward task. How can you recognize a good one when you see it? This is the critical decision for the entrepreneurial team utilizing the spin-up model.

In general, a good technology should have solid proof of a principle and a benchtop prototype. The path to raise its TRL should be relatively clear, even though it has not been done yet. There should also be a very clear and definite commitment from the inventor to be involved in the technology development process as an advisor or chief technology officer. You should have some reasonable belief that the technology will do what the inventor says it will, that it is scalable, and that it solves some real-life problem.

The technology should not have any obvious IP obstacles. A preliminary Internet search for possible blocking or competing patents should be undertaken using key words for the technology as search terms. This search can provide a quick look at obvious potential IP obstacles, but it is not a substitute for a full patent search prepared by patent counsel. If it appears to be relatively close to other patents in the same subject matter area, there is a risk of being tied up in patent litigation. If all of the

---

[4] "The Bayh-Dole Act: It's Working." n.d. AUTM website. www.autm.net/ AM/Template.cfm?Section=Bayh_Dole_Act&Template=/CM/ContentDisplay. cfm&ContentID=11603 (accessed May 21, 2015).

preliminary indicators for the technology look good, then a full patent search should be completed a bit later in the process prior to a permanent license agreement. In addition to the technology having no obvious IP obstacles, the patent should have been filed reasonably recently with a good priority date.

A preliminary Internet search of potentially competing or analogous devices or technologies or both will help determine what the potential competitive advantage of your technology might be. In general, there should be some idea of where it fits in the overall supply chain, who the end user might be, and who the actual target purchaser might be, given the position of the technology in an overall product cycle. Even at this early stage, the spin-up SME should have an idea of the competitive advantage that can be exploited from the technology. Usually, competitive advantage criteria are the standard categories of quicker, better, or cheaper—all of which add up to some additional value to the end user from the adoption of the technology.

An evaluation of an early-stage technology should also include an overview of the drivers and potential obstacles for market adoption. Government regulation or certification can drive the market to adopt new technologies or can impose such long time frames for approval that it is very difficult to bring the technology to market. The heart of the spin-up model is the ability to raise the TRL of a technology and bring it to market faster than a spinout or start-up. Therefore, we advise staying away from technologies like pharma, biotech, some environmental devices, and some medical devices when using the spin-up model.

It would also be helpful if the technology can be described relatively simply to a knowledgeable layperson. This allows for clear marketing messages to potential funders and ultimately to targets and end users.

The critical inflection point for the formation of a spin-up is the correct evaluation of a technology to determine if it can be matured in conformance to market requirements. Often the very early stage of its development makes it very hard for any business to recognize its potential or to risk investment in developing it. Judging the actual stage of development and the amount of development required are critical elements of any business plan for a spin-up SME.

The National Aeronautics and Space Administration (NASA), the U.S. space agency, has developed the standard categories for technology

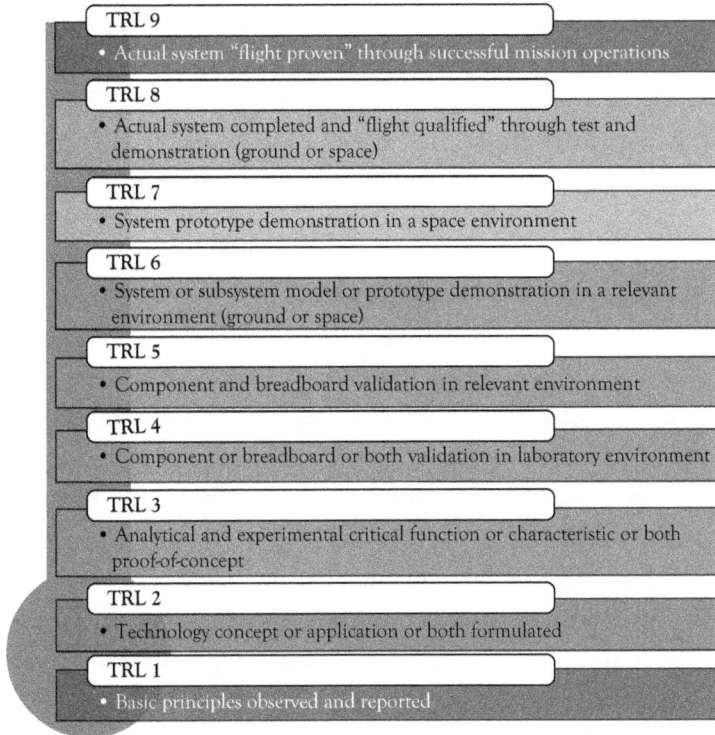

TRL 9
• Actual system "flight proven" through successful mission operations

TRL 8
• Actual system completed and "flight qualified" through test and demonstration (ground or space)

TRL 7
• System prototype demonstration in a space environment

TRL 6
• System or subsystem model or prototype demonstration in a relevant environment (ground or space)

TRL 5
• Component and breadboard validation in relevant environment

TRL 4
• Component or breadboard or both validation in laboratory environment

TRL 3
• Analytical and experimental critical function or characteristic or both proof-of-concept

TRL 2
• Technology concept or application or both formulated

TRL 1
• Basic principles observed and reported

Figure 5.2 Technology readiness levels used by NASA

Abbreviation: NASA, National Aeronautics and Space Administration.

development. These categories are referred to as TRLs, as shown in Figure 5.2 (see www.nasa.gov/content/technology-readiness-level/). The University of Southern California's Marshall School of Business provides a set of TRLs for a variety of different technological areas at www.usc. edu/org/techalliance/pdf/CTC_TRI_Definitions-2007.pdf. A standard web search will discover many discussions of TRLs for most categories of technology.

Market-ready technologies are typically at TRL 6 or higher. Most often, early-stage technologies that are available for licensing are at TRLs 2 through 4. In most cases, we recommend that a spin-up entrepreneur should not consider working with any technology less than a TRL 4, unless they are certain that it might be "the best thing since sliced bread." In such a case, a TRL 3 might be an acceptable risk. For that once-in-a-lifetime opportunity, a TRL 2 might be considered. The risk associated with any technology is astronomically larger if you cannot "kick the tires" to check it out in fact, which is typically at TRL 4. In mapping out the transition to TRL 6, the spin-up company will need to plan out all of the required technical development steps, resources, budget, and the estimated time for completion.

Team

Successful teams engage in two critical activities. First, they must recognize commercially valuable early-stage technologies and then successfully gain control of exclusive rights to the technology for the development maturation process. Second, after moving the technology up the TRL, they must sell this improved innovation asset to other companies. These two critical activities help define the skills and qualities required in assembling the right team.

The importance of the team cannot be overstated. The conventional wisdom among angel investors is that it is much better to invest in a great team with a mediocre technology than in a great technology with a mediocre team.

A spin-up company entrepreneurial team must correctly select a technology or group of technologies for development by combining entrepreneurial market information and technical expertise. The scientist inventor can provide the required level of technical understanding, but it is a rare scientist who can also provide the business or entrepreneurial skills required.

Some scientists decide to become entrepreneurs, but for most, this is a difficult transition. The success of a spin-up, start-up, or spinout will be determined by accomplishing tasks better undertaken by entrepreneurs. This dilemma was clearly stated in an article on commercialization in the *Chemical & Engineering News*: "Many scientists intrinsically understand that their discoveries might translate into important, highly profitable entrepreneurial enterprises," says Madeleine Jacobs, executive director and CEO of the American Chemical Society, which published a report in 2011 on chemical entrepreneurs (*C&EN*, November 7, 2011, page 47). "But making a discovery or patenting an invention is only the beginning of creating a company. Bringing that idea or invention to commercialization and creating a successful company requires a different set of skills and knowledge than carrying out basic research."[5] This is why, in most cases, the scientist inventor will decide to maintain his or her status as a researcher. The scientist inventor will often provide technical expertise through acting as an advisor or chief technical officer on a part-time basis. Continuity on the scientific side most often comes from including a graduate or postgraduate student who has worked on the technology as PI on the spin-up team.

In addition to technical or scientific skills, the team must include marketing and business skills. One person may have more than one of these skills, but it is highly unlikely that a single person can perform all the tasks required for success.

One of the key skills required is the ability to interact with potential users and lead customers at the earliest-possible stage in the project. These interactions will be critical to the adoption of the technology at a later stage. Adoption of new innovative technology

> results from a series of individual decisions to begin using the new technology, decisions which are often the result of a comparison of the uncertain benefits of the new invention with the uncertain costs of adopting it. An understanding of the factors affecting this choice is essential . . . for the creators and producers of such technologies.[6]

This interaction with the potential end users and target customers is an essential aspect of moving quickly and seamlessly into the market. Therefore, there is value in including entrepreneurs or business development staff who have existing industry experience and contacts as team members.

---

[5] Morrissey, S.R. 2012. "What Researchers Who Want to Be Entrepreneurs Need to Know." *Chemical & Engineering News*, August 20, 2012. http://cen.acs.org/articles/90/i34/Researchers-Want-Entrepreneurs-Need-Know.html

[6] Hall, B., and B. Khan. 2002. "Adoption of New Technology." *New Economy Handbook: Holland and Khan*. University of California Berkley. http://eml.berkeley.edu/~bhhall/papers/HallKhan03%20diffusion.pdf (accessed May 21, 2015).

There is a certain mythology about technology companies that portrays the founders as almost universally young people, primarily university dropouts who create brilliant new companies. While there is an element of truth in this mythology in the Internet software sector, it is not an accurate statement across the board for all technology SMEs, including spin-ups. The skills required for the spin-up entrepreneur are real-life business experience, professional training, and the ability to interact with potential clients, which can often only be obtained over time. Therefore, it would be a mistake to exclude people with business skills from the spin-up team simply due to age. The issue of age and entrepreneurship was examined in a recent study by the Kauffman Foundation, which found that the peak age for entrepreneurial activity is age 40 and that high-tech start-ups are twice as likely to be founded by someone older than age 50, as opposed to someone younger than 25.[7]

Once it is understood who should be a member of the spin-up team, the question is how to find the required people who are not already part of the team. The commercialization process for early-stage technologies is most successful in places with a full and active "innovation ecosystem" that includes a pool of people with the skills required. The term innovation ecosystem is borrowed from biology to represent a balanced and mutually reinforcing collection of high-quality research institutions, serial entrepreneurs, financing at levels varying from seed to angel to venture, industry or sector professional organizations, supportive state agencies, physical facilities for small companies, and services for legal, accounting, marketing, and mentoring. All of these merge and interact in complex patterns that facilitate matching researchers, technologies, and entrepreneurs to create commercially successful SMEs of all sorts. This mixing process takes part formally and informally through the plethora of agencies, trade organizations, and networking events that characterize a sophisticated innovation ecosystem.

---

[7] Wiens, J., and E. Fetsch. February 25, 2015. "Demographic Trends Will Shape the Future of Entrepreneurship." The Kauffman Foundation. www.kauffman.org/what-we-do/resources/entrepreneurship-policy-digest/demographic-trends-will-shape-the-future-of-entrepreneurship

Where no such ecosystem exists to pair entrepreneurs with technologies, it is much harder to match technologies with entrepreneurial teams. This leads to a buildup of technologies without any route to market, which is often the case in many midsize and smaller universities and research hospitals and in government labs and nonprofit research facilities. As a consequence, there is a relatively large pool of technologies that have never been adequately evaluated for their actual commercial potential, which creates a problem for these institutions and a potential opportunity for the entrepreneur looking for spin-up opportunities. Often, this commercial potential lies in applications of which the inventor was unaware. Recognition of the key role of a mutually supportive innovation ecosphere is increasingly driving policy and programs for economic development. The contradiction remains between the opportunity for the discovery of unexamined gems of technology and the difficulties of development in an undeveloped innovation ecosystem.

The simplified objective of the spin-up SME and the real measure of success of the team is realization of profit. With this in mind, an important aspect of assembling the team is finding people who embrace this objective and then incentivizing them properly. Spin-ups, like spinouts and start-ups, typically do not have much in the way of operating funds and what they have should be dedicated to the development process. This means that the incentive for the staff is usually a combination of salary at some relatively low level and a share in future profits through share ownership in the spin-up company.

Allocation of share ownership or potential to earn share ownership is a balancing act that all spin-ups must perform. There are a number of interests that must be accommodated through first-level stock distributions and incentive-based stock options. Beyond the question of incentivizing the team, the spin-up will most likely have other claims on equity, ranging from the holders of the IP for the early-stage technology to subsequent funding rounds that will continually require rebalancing equity interests.

Universities, university research foundations, research hospitals, or federal laboratories hold the rights to a majority of early-stage technologies. As part of the licensing agreement, these rights holders will sometimes ask for equity in the SME as part of the license agreement. Different research institutions have different policies regarding holding shares in SMEs to which they license technologies. Some universities and research hospitals balance requiring lower royalty fees against the opportunity to hold shares in the SME. Some like Carnegie Mellon, Massachusetts Institute of Technology (MIT), and Stanford hold up to 5 to 6 percent equity that they will hold until bought out as part of the first financing event for the SME holding the license. Others like the University of Texas at Austin require even larger equity shares in the SME, with no obligation to sell. On the other hand, government labs almost never take equity shares and many nonprofits prefer not to, as part of their license agreements.

Once any equity has been apportioned to the rights holder, the remaining equity should be allocated in various proportions to the founders, the entrepreneurial leader, the inventor, the PI, and possibly other key staff members. Each situation is different, so there is no real standard division of equity. Furthermore, the equity shares are likely to be changed, diluted, or superseded in subsequent rounds of financing as part of the terms required by lenders. The founding entrepreneurial team will want to hold on to as much equity as possible for as long as possible but should not expect no dilution of their shares as the project goes through rounds of financing. The spin-up management should engage experienced legal business counsel to assist in drawing up bylaws and shareholder agreements at the earliest-possible stage.

Market Intelligence

Preliminary market research is critical to deciding whether to undertake a spin-up project. The objective of this research is to make an educated guess about the market utility of the technology. Put another way, if the spin-up SME can successfully raise the TRL of the technology, will it make money for the SME?

Assuming that your due diligence indicates that the new technology does what the inventor says it can do, is there any potential market demand? This may not be as simple a question to answer as it appears because sometimes the market utility is found in contexts other than the experimental purpose for which it was conceived. Sometimes you may be looking at a platform technology that requires finding the best application.

Determining whether the technology has market utility requires a determination of whether it solves a real problem that no other technology has solved, or whether it can displace an existing technology by performing the same function better, faster, or cheaper. If so, then we can expect that there will be market demand and potential profit provided that it can be competitive in the market.

To be competitive, it must include the physical or technical characteristics to conform to market standards that will assure easy adoption. Many of the technologies that would fit within our model for spin-ups will either improve existing processes or be subassembly or replacement devices or processes within a much larger technological system. This means that as the TRL is raised, the technology will be compatible with larger systems and thus make it easier to adopt.

Ultimately, market research and intelligence will lead to estimates of what the market price could be for the spin-up technology, that is, what potential end users would expect to pay and what potential acquirers would expect to pay. The ability to produce a new technology that can actually enter the market depends upon whether it can be produced at a market-competitive price, relative to its competition. As difficult as it is to project ultimate costs and utility at the initial stage of a spin-up, there must be enough preliminary data to support a projection of successfully satisfying market demand at a reasonable and competitive price.

Preliminary research should include broad Internet searches for market size, competitors, and principal companies in the sector that might want to acquire the spin-up technology.

Determining market size for the spin-up technology poses very difficult problems in assessing the real market for component technologies. Internet searches will often turn up many multiclient industry research reports prepared by large consulting companies like Frost & Sullivan. While these may be a useful starting point, the portion of the report that is publically available is usually too broad in scope to provide the level of specific market information required. The spin-up research needs to narrowly focus on the specific market size for the actual technology. For instance, the market for an improved gas temperature measurement device for gas turbine generators is not the same as the total size of the market for gas turbine generators. Start-ups often incorrectly exaggerate the potential market size as part of their fund-raising efforts, but a spin-up cannot afford to make this mistake in evaluating the market demand for its technology.

Similarly, the research into competitors must be objective and thorough. We often encounter inventors who state that they have no competitors. This is almost never the case. Usually the inventor is solving a known problem using a different method than commonly employed by industry. So while there may not be a competitor who does the exact same thing, there is usually any number of competitors who are already in the market. The spin-up entrepreneur must understand exactly who these competitors are and what potential competitive advantage the new technology may possess. If the new technology truly has competitive advantage, then a competitor could also become a potential acquirer of the new technology to strengthen its own market position.

It is also critical to understand the supply chain for the spin-up technology to determine the exact point of insertion and the potential acquirers. Since spin-up technologies are often improvements for existing processes or equipment, the end user of the product may not be the actual potential acquirer. The real target for sale of the improved TRL technology will often be an intermediate manufacturer or service provider.

Not only should the spin-up team identify potential acquirers but, in many cases, should attempt to speak with them directly as early as possible in the development cycle. Often the target for licensing of the developed technology will not be the end user but may be a manufacturer, supplier, or wholesaler. Thus, targets may be competitors or may be the potential licensor or acquirer of the technology. At the initial stage, the entrepreneur should be directly engaged with both potential users and potential targets in order to gauge the practical commercial potential for the technology. The initial purpose of this contact should be to determine the level of "pain" or market demand that might exist for the new technology and the characteristics that it needs to have for market adoption. These early contacts can also lead to establishing development partnerships and to later monetization of the upgraded TRL technology.

As another component of market analysis, the spin-up team needs to understand the kind of regulatory review or certification that will be required to bring the new technology to market. The team must determine the approximate cost and general time period required to complete these processes. Since the general purpose of the spin-up model is to provide an accelerated path to market, we would advise avoiding biotech, pharma, and some types of environmental technology that require extensive testing, review, and certification.

In the context of industrial and business activity, market utility means determining whether it may be possible to generate new income for the entity acquiring the technology from deploying the invention. Those inventions that can generate additional income can be marketed as assets for acquisition. This is the goal of the spin-up SME. Accurate and objective market intelligence is a key component of this determination.

Funding

The final piece of the development process is funding. Once a team has been assembled, initial license terms established, and a technology development plan created, it will be possible to estimate the overhead, time to completion, and combined budget. At this stage, the team must identify the sources of funding that will be sufficient to carry them through the development period for raising the TRL to reach the exit stage of profitable monetization of the technology.

In devising the business plan and budget for raising the TRL rating of the technology, the spin-up team should be aware of the general contours of various alternative funding sources. The actual financial plan will differ greatly from spin-up to spin-up, but the component parts are most likely virtually the same for all of them.

Fortunately for entrepreneurs, sources of funding for innovative technologies have continued to expand in parallel with the evolution of open innovation and the increasing availability of new technologies from universities and government labs. These new sources of funding include federal and state government programs that support innovative small business, corporate investment funds, angel investors, venture capital investors, and the newest potential source of investment, crowdsourcing.

Augmenting these sources of funding is an increasingly diverse set of business plan competitions, technology parks, technology accelerators, incubators, and innovation zones. Some of these innovative small business support institutions are government supported, some are private businesses, and some are owned by nonprofit organizations. The number and diversity of these organizations is increasing dramatically with many of them offering some kind of preseed investment, seed-level investment, or grant funding.

Business plan competitions have become so prevalent that it is impossible to even list a sampling without missing some important competition. For an example of one website purporting to be the largest listing site, go to www.bizplancompetitions.com/competitions/. Many of these competitions are now focused on specific technology sectors as well. The utility of business plan competitions is usually not the prize money awarded but the exposure to the broader technology and investment communities clustered around these competitions, which gives them the character of technology accelerators. Many of the competitions are not geographically limited in who can participate. See, for instance, Mass Challenge, which claims to be the largest business accelerator program in the world and which draws competitors from around the world (http://masschallenge.org).

Technology accelerators are spreading throughout the United States and becoming fixtures in the tech community.[8] One study rated the top three as AngelPad in San Francisco (www.angelpad.com), Mucker Lab in Los Angeles (www.muckercapital.com), and Techstars in various locations (www.techstars.com).[9] One of the most famous U.S. accelerators Y Combinator is now considered a seed fund.[10]

In the United States, there is an increasing development of innovation districts in urban centers in cities like Atlanta, Baltimore, Buffalo, Cambridge, Cleveland, Detroit, Houston, Philadelphia, Pittsburgh, St. Louis, and San Diego. They are also developing in Boston, Brooklyn, Chicago, Portland, Providence, San Francisco, and Seattle where

---

[8] Solomon, B. 2015. "The Best Startup Accelerators of 2015." *Forbes Magazine Online*, May 17. www.forbes.com/sites/briansolomon/2015/03/17/the-best-startup-accelerators-of-2015-powering-a-tech-boom/ (accessed August 5, 2015).

[9] Solomon (2015).

[10] Solomon (2015).

older industrial areas are being remade as innovation districts.[11] Some of these new innovation districts offer funding or support programs that are location specific and as such may influence the location of the spin-up company. An example of this type of support is the nonprofit organization, JumpStart, headquartered in Cleveland and providing funding support for start-up companies in Northeast Ohio (www.jump-startinc.org/).

It is important to understand that all of these evolving support structures for innovative, technology-oriented companies are supplemental and support based. The true test of survival for a new technology company and particularly a spin-up company is whether it can raise sufficient public or private funding to cover its expenses during the development period, a time in a company's life sometimes referred to as the "valley of death." Can the company manage to raise sufficient financial resources to prevent death by a lack of operating funds? The answer to this question is usually found in whether or not the company can successful tap programs like the Small Business Innovation Research (SBIR) program, the Small Business Technology Transfer (STTR) programs in the United States, or their international analogues.

SBIR and STTR Programs and Equivalent Programs

One of the principal sources of financing for early-stage companies in the United States is through the SBIR grant program. This program offers competitive grants in phased awards to support the development and commercialization of U.S. applied science. The STTR program is a companion to SBIR and supports research collaborations between small companies and federal research labs.

---

[11] Katz, B., and J. Wagner. 2014. "The Rise of Innovation Districts—A New Geography of Innovation in America." Brookings Institute. www.brookings. edu/about/programs/metro/innovation-districts?utm_campaign=Metropoli tan+Policy+Program&utm_source=hs_email&utm_medium=email&utm_ content=13125549&_hsenc=p2ANqtz-9mYGGY8AM8hESRQKulOaT-BmENswXTmn8edUdW18MveEe2v9FXZddhljj_Ff3j0r-gQW4dDcN-0F32JtQ9YhYh49fTF49iwlrYbS_S3K1wlpQmqDEFE&_hsmi=13125549

The SBIR program was established with the passing of the Small Business Innovation Development Act in 1982 to award federal research grants to small businesses. The Act obligates federal agencies that spend more than $100 million per year for outside R&D to allocate a fixed proportion of that funding, now 2.8 percent, to small business grants. Currently, 11 federal agencies participate in the SBIR program, with the largest number of grants coming from the Department of Defense.[12] Winners of SBIR Phase I grants can receive up to $150,000 in grant funding for a six-month period and Phase 2 grants can go up to $1 million for a two-year period.[13]

These grants funds provide nondilutive financing for early-stage technologies that otherwise would have great difficulty receiving financing at this stage. Therefore, this source of funding is strategically important for the spin-up model in the United States.

Similar programs have been implemented around the world. The British government has its own version of SBIR called the Small Business Research Initiative, which began in 2001. Other European governments and the European Union (EU) have developed SBIR-like programs to promote innovation through the support of SMEs. For a summary of various types of seed and early-stage funding in the 34 Organization for Economic Co-operation and Development (OECD) countries, see OECD Science, Technology and Industry Policy Papers, No. 9, "Policies for Seed and Early Stage Finance: Findings from the 2012 OECD Financing Questionnaire," prepared by Karen Wilson and Filipe Silva and published in 2013 (http://dx.doi.org/10.1787/5k3xqsf00j33-en). Canada has the Idea to Innovation Program www.ic.gc.ca/eic/site/054.nsf/eng/00112.html. Chile has the Production Development Program known by its Spanish acronym CORFO (www2.corfo.cl). Singapore has SPRING Singapore (www.spring.gov.sg). These are just representative samples of similar government early-stage support funds that have proliferated in many countries.

---

[12] "About SBIR." n.d. SBIR website. www.sbir.gov/about/about-sbir (accessed June 2, 2015).

[13] "About SBIR." n.d. SBIR website. www.sbir.gov/about/about-sbir (accessed June 2, 2015).

Corporate Investment

The development of corporate contacts is an extension of the market intelligence conducted as part of the initial screening of the technology and should be considered as a critical success element in marketing and exit strategy. Corporate venture funds are proliferating around the world and becoming a critical element of the open innovation strategy of global companies. Between 2010 and 2014, the number of these companies increased by 475 new companies to reach a total of around 1,100.[14] The largest corporate venture fund is Google, but many other major international companies have companion corporate investment funds to invest in new technologies, including Intel Capital, GE Ventures, Samsung Venture Investment, Siemens Venture Capital, SingTel Innov8, SoftBank Capital, and many others.[15]

As indicated earlier in this chapter, corporations remain interested in obtaining innovative practical implementation of basic science, despite their declining internal R&D funding.[16] The resolution of these contradictory tendencies is their continuing interest in acquiring the developed fruits of scientific innovation in the form of higher-level TRL technologies. Keeping in mind that the real goal of the spin-up SME is to profitably divest itself of the technology through licensing or sale of the company, early involvement with potential company targets is critically important.

The SBIR program specifically recognizes the utility of this early involvement as one of its criteria for Phase 2 awards. The applicant needs to show industry support as proof of the commercial potential for the technology. Corporate involvement at this point can include a wide range

[14] Rahal, R. December 15, 2014. "Will Corporate Venture Capital Disrupt the Traditional Investment Ecosystem?" Entrepreneur website. www.entrepreneur.com/article/240904, (accessed August 5, 2015).

[15] Zipkin, N. July 10, 2014. "Google Ventures Launches $100 Million Startup Fund in Europe." Entrepreneur website. www.entrepreneur.com/article/235510 (accessed August 5, 2015).

[16] Arora, A., S. Belenzon, and A. Patacconi. January 2015. "Killing the Golden Goose? The Decline of Science in Corporate R&D." National Bureau of Economic Research, Working Paper 20902. www.nber.org/papers/w20902

of potential activities including joint research, testing of prototypes, seed funding, and review of product characteristics.

Angel Investors

Functionally, angel investors provide equity funding at an early stage of technology and company development. Although there is a great deal of business media buzz about venture capital companies, they typically do not invest in early-stage technologies and are not particularly relevant to the spin-up model company.

The term "angel" originally comes from Broadway, where it was used to describe wealthy individuals who provided money for theatrical productions. In 1978, William Wetzel, then a professor at the University of New Hampshire and founder of its Center for Venture Research, completed a pioneering study on how entrepreneurs raised seed capital in the United States, and he began using the term angel to describe the investors that supported them.[17]

Generally speaking, an angel investor or angel is an affluent individual who provides capital for a business start-up, usually in exchange for convertible debt or ownership equity. As opposed to nondilutive grant funding from SBIR programs or their analogues, angel investors will expect to take an ownership interest in the spin-up SME. From a financial point of view, angel financing can reduce the return to the original founders of the SME but may be beneficial from other points of view. Often, angel investors are retired executives or successful entrepreneurs with specialized sector expertise or industry sector contacts that could be critical to the spin-up, in addition to providing funds to bridge the valley of death.

As a general matter, angel investors tend to be very locally focused and hands-on with their investments. This means that the spin-up SME seeking angel funding will need to carefully screen the angel to make sure that they can work together and that the angel buys into the specific business model of the spin-up. It also means that it is pretty unrealistic to expect

---

[17] "Angel Investor." *Wikipedia.* http://en.wikipedia.org/wiki/Angel_investor (accessed June 3, 2015).

angel funding from someone outside the immediate driving distance of the spin-up location.

Venture Capital

Venture capital is a specialized outgrowth of small business lending but one focused on taking equity in the new small business. Typically, venture capitalists are interested in larger investments at a later stage of development than angel investors.

One of the first steps toward a professionally managed venture capital industry was the passage of the Small Business Investment Act of 1958. The 1958 Act officially allowed the U.S. Small Business Administration to license private small business investment companies to facilitate financing and management of small entrepreneurial businesses in the United States. These companies evolved into what we now know as venture capital firms.

During the 1960s and 1970s, venture capital firms focused their investment activity primarily on starting and expanding companies. More often than not, these companies were exploiting breakthroughs in electronic, medical, or data-processing technology. As a result, venture capital came to be almost synonymous with technology finance.

Venture capital played an instrumental role in developing many of the major technology companies of the 1980s. Some of the most notable venture capital investments were made in firms that include Tandem Computers, Genentech, Apple Inc., Electronic Arts, Compaq, Federal Express, and LSI Corporation.[18]

Today, the traditional model of venture capital is under examination, with fewer companies operating successfully and increasing competition from angel investors, as the actual costs of forming new companies and maturing technologies decline.

---

[18] Powers, J. February 20, 2012. "The History of Private Equity and Venture Capital." Corporate Live Wire. www.corporatelivewire.com/top-story.html?id=the-history-of-private-equity-venture-capital (accessed January 11, 2015).

Crowdfunding

Over the past decade or so, crowdsourcing has developed as a particular form of open innovation that relies on individuals around the world linked by the Internet. In a seminal article in *Wired* in 2006, Jeff Howe defined the new phenomena of crowdsourcing. In that article, he noted:

> Technological advances in everything from product design software to digital video cameras are breaking down the cost barriers that once separated amateurs from professionals. Hobbyists, part-timers, and dabblers suddenly have a market for their efforts, as smart companies in industries as disparate as pharmaceuticals and television discover ways to tap the latent talent of the crowd. The labor isn't always free, but it costs a lot less than paying traditional employees. It's not outsourcing; it's crowdsourcing.[19]

Along with crowdsourcing as a source of resources for companies, a parallel process of crowdfunding emerged as an innovative new form of finance, also powered by the Internet.

In practice, crowdfunding is actually a complicated amalgam of different kinds of finance, each with a different consequence for the spin-up entrepreneur. See Figure 5.3 for a simplified listing of types of crowdfunding and the return to funders. The term itself has become very popular, and the practice of crowdfunding has become a critical success factor for some projects. Given the popular use of the term and the confusion about the different consequences from different types of crowdfunding, it is worthwhile to carefully delineate each type. The different types of crowdfunding are differentiated by their function and by the return expected by those who participate.

One of the most visible types of crowdfunding is project based, notably through Internet platforms like Kickstarter (www.kickstarter.com) and Indiegogo (www.indiegogo.com). Kickstarter was founded in 2009, and by 2013, more than 5 million people had participated, with more than 1.5 million in more than one project. Some of the projects funded through Kickstarter have raised large sums of money, but the majority still

---

[19] Howe, J. June 2006. "The Rise of Crowdsourcing." *Wired.* http://archive.wired.com/wired/archive/14.06/crowds.html (accessed June 5, 2015).

Lending based	Reward based	Donation based	Equity based
Investors receive a return of principal and interest.	Investors receive acknowledgment, a product, a service, or an award.	Investors donate for charity or to show moral support.	Investors receive shares in the company.

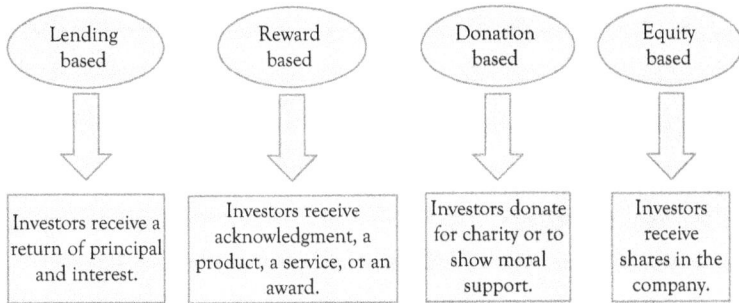

Figure 5.3 Types of crowdfunding

is in the $10,000 range.[20] Indiegogo promotes itself as the world's largest funding website, with the broadest number of categories of funding campaigns. Sampling these two sites only scratches the surface of an exploding number of Internet fund-raising websites. There have been a progressively larger and larger number of websites that allow for the aggregation of small amounts of money as the source of funding for activities ranging from financing independent music production to the production of three-dimensional (3D) printers and every conceivable project in between.

In recent years, the practice of crowdfunding has become a prominent source of funding for innovative technology projects, like, for example, 3D printers. A 2014 article in *3D Printing Digest* highlights 3D printers as one of the most active categories for crowdfunding, highlighting 10 highly successful projects. One example cited was the 3Doodler, a 3D printing pen that requested $30,000 and ultimately raised $2.3 million on Kickstarter.[21] In considering this type of funding, the spin-up company should keep in mind that this is project-oriented funding, not equity finance. Acknowledgments, discounted products or services, or creative awards compensate the large number of contributors. Others are strictly making a donation.

Another type of crowdfunding is lending based in which the parties making the loans expect repayment with interest from the borrower. One of the examples of this kind of crowdfunding is Lending Tree (www.lendingtree.

---

[20] McGregor, M., and F. Benenson. October 29, 2013. "Five Million Backers!" Kickstarter Blog. www.kickstarter.com/blog/five-million-backers (accessed June 5, 2015).
[21] Fred. February 21, 2014. "The 10 Top Crowdfunded 3D Printers on Kickstarter." *3D Printing Digest.* http://3dprintingdigest.com/10-top-crowdfunded-3d-printers-kickstarter/72/ (accessed June 5, 2015).

com/?esourceid=5344230&800num=800-461-0117&cchannel=sem
&csource=msn&cmethod=search&cname=branded&ccontent=d&
cterm=lending+tree&PPCKW=lending+tree&ADID=1485316649).
This type of crowdfunding is targeted toward consumer finance and is
not particularly relevant for the spin-up company.

The final type of crowdfunding is equity based. This sort of funding
has been forbidden by the United States but is in the process of changing. Ever since the Great Depression in the 1930s, the U.S. Security and
Exchange Commission (SEC) has strictly regulated the sale of equity
shares, requiring registration for public sale and preventing anyone other
than a "qualified investor" from investing in private equity investment.
Angel investors are able to invest in small companies and receive equity
because they are qualified investors.

In late March 2012, the U.S. Congress passed the Jumpstart Our
Business Startups Act, better known by its acronym, the JOBS Act. This
legislation was intended to provide an exception to SEC rules to allow for
equity crowdfunding. Implementation of this Act depends upon issuance
of a new set of rules by the SEC. These have not yet been issued as of the
date of writing of this chapter.

Even before implementation, there has been a lot of controversy about
the real impact of equity crowdfunding. Some venture investors are ada-
mantly opposed to participating in any crowdfunded company because
they would have enormously increased corporate overhead with diverse
and numerous shareholders.

Meanwhile, Europe has pushed ahead of the United States with significant crowdfunding platforms in the United Kingdom, Germany,
France, and Switzerland. The Swiss and U.K. platforms offer equity shares
in companies, while the others are loan or holding company based.[22]

As the rules for equity crowdfunding become clear and different models
emerge in different countries, the spin-up company will have to consider
carefully the full range of consequences for such funding before engaging.

---

[22] "Crowdfunding for Equity in Europe: Which Platforms Are Bringing in the
Most Money?" March 13, 2015. Rude Baguette website. www.rudebaguette.
com/2015/03/13/crowdfunding-equity-europe-platforms-bringing-money/
(accessed August 5, 2015).

However, crowdfunding is expected to grow as a broad popular format for investment that should be investigated for possible spin-up funding.

Exit Strategy

The distinguishing characteristic of the spin-up model for SMEs is the declared intention to exit through licensing or sale of the rights to the technology at the earliest-possible stage. The growing adoption of open innovation approaches by multinational and large companies makes this exit strategy more and more possible.

The biggest danger to this exit strategy comes from success in raising the TRL rating of the technology. As the TRL rises, there will be an inevitable tendency to push it just a little bit farther than time or funding allows. An even greater risk will come from the temptation to change the model and become a real operating company.

As the spin-up SME begins to achieve technological success, the company leadership will need to exercise a disciplined approach to the original exit strategy. They will need to correctly evaluate when and to whom to license the technology. They will need a very disciplined approach to the exit in order to maximize return for all the stakeholders within a reasonable time period. It is at this point that technological success can lead to commercial greed.

In start-ups that are intended to become operating companies as either producers or service companies, there is usually a point at which the original leadership has to give way to new leadership. The original leadership carries the company through a certain stage of its development, but they do not have the skills for the next stage. Often this transition is precipitated by outside funding from venture capital or angel investors who insist upon executive change as part of the additional financing rounds.

In the spin-up model, the ideal situation would be to have no outside equity funding and to exit from the technology within a relatively short period of time, meaning from two to four years. The spin-up leadership team has been constructed for this objective and not to build an operating company. Operating within the model, there should not be any inherent need for a change in leadership, provided that the team has the discipline to fulfill the model as planned.

The mechanics of an exit through licensing or sale of the company are not a mystery; however, the art of a successful spin-up exit strategy will depend upon correctly timing the exit and keeping a clear hold on the model.

The monetization of the company will come as either a long-term revenue stream from licensing fees that are divided among the original stakeholders according to the original terms of the deal or through proportional shares in the sale price of the technology as a whole.

Conclusion: Fundamental Success Factors for a Spin-Up Business Model

Assuming that any monetization event may take from two to four years, entrepreneurs need to carefully choose the technologies to commercialize under a spin-up model. It is critical to pay attention to all success factors in order to minimize risk and maximize the possibility of success. The following success factors need careful consideration:

1. Choose technology properly. Coldly and objectively, evaluate any technology being considered for spin-up in terms of its potential for commercialization and potential financial reward. Minimum screening criteria should include the following:

    a. Qualify a pool of technologies for which you know there is market demand or a market opening that has been identified through your own research. From this pool, involve industry experts in a second-level review, with the full range of analysis to pick a very limited number from this pool.

    b. Get to know the inventor and the current owner of the IP to find out whether they lack some critical capability to commercialize the technology on their own and therefore will be willing to work through the spin-up mechanism.

    c. Find out whether the inventor and current owner of the IP will be willing to extend a no-cost option to license or no-cost license to a new spin-up legal entity.

    d. Confirm that there is a PI with the sector technical expertise and competency to manage the development of the technology.

      e. Select technologies that will not require extensive regulatory approval, meaning the exclusion of pharmaceuticals, medical equipment, and some technologies regulated by the Environment Protection Agency (EPA) because of the time to market required by the regulatory process.

      f. Review the development plan to confirm that there is a reasonable prospect that the spin-up process can be completed within two to four years.

2. Human resources. Make sure that the spin-up company team includes people who can manage the science and technology development and who can provide business-oriented skills in marketing and target management.

3. Process map for the spin-up technical development. Prepare cost estimates and an evaluation of the technical capacity required. At the initial stage, the spin-up will need at least an outline of the technical tasks that need to be accomplished to raise the TRL, the resources necessary to accomplish those tasks, and a timeline projection for completion.

    A very important aspect of a spin-up model is the time horizon for expected returns. The time horizon impacts the expense level for maintaining the hands-on staff resources and overhead, therefore determining the level of finance needed and sources of funds at each particular stage of development. It is critical to be able to map out the milestones and match those with capabilities, resources, and funding sources to determine whether to enter into the spin-up process.

4. Financial support for development. Identify the source of funding for each stage of technology development, whether government (SBIR and STTR), financial investor (primarily an Angel or a group of Angels), state or local development agency, or industry partner. There are increasingly diverse sources of funding for start-up companies, but except for the SBIR and STTR funding, much of the available funding (including private) is tied to particular localities. This will also be a factor in your financial planning. This is the famous "valley of death" problem for any new technology. A spin-up will have to explore some combination of SBIR and STTR grants,

industry partnerships, and angel equity finance to move technologies up the TRL. In this, a spin-up is no different than any other similar type of organization.

5. Exit strategy. Having a credible and disciplined exit plan that will result in either a long-term license for the technology or a sale of the spin-up company is a critical element of any successful strategy. The goal is always to monetize the technology through improving the TRL of the technology and disposing of it.

CHAPTER 6

Conclusion

Phyllis Speser, JD, PhD, RTTP

There is a reason small and medium enterprises (SMEs) are called for-profit companies. Your number one job is to generate profits. Profits get divided up between shareholders, employees, and sometimes contractors, vendors, charities, and others. In short, when there is more money to go around, that is a good thing. So far, we told you nothing that you did not already know.

Hopefully, you have found this book helpful because you realize the tools it describes can be used to make bigger profits. We have presented five tools: (1) crowdsourcing, (2) technology transfer, (3) brokers, (4) auctions, and (5) spin-ups. There are other tools, of course. These are good ones to get started with because they have been proven in practice by SMEs to lead to greater profits when doing open innovation.

Open innovation addresses two things SMEs need to do to make profits: Have products or services to sell, and the legal right to make, use, and sell those products or services.

Every industry has a product life cycle. With increasing globalization of competition, product life cycles are running shorter. You have a "make or buy" decision. Develop the product in-house or use open innovation. Open innovation can deliver enhancements for this generation's products and technology to build products for the next generation and the generation after it.

Because of the global glut of technology, it is a great time to be a buyer. Technology is inexpensive. Even better, most countries have government subsidies to support applied research and development (R&D) and product development. Only small companies can tap many of these subsidies. For SMEs, the economics of the make-buy decision with respect to new product and process technology has changed dramatically.

It is business 101 that the profit you can make depends on the cost of technology or intellectual property (IP) acquisition, the cost of technology and product development, and the sales price for the final product (or the licensing fees charged for the IP covering the technology). There are, by the way, known ways of calculating a rough estimate of the fair market value of a technology and its associated IP. The fair market value is paid out through up-front fees, milestone payments, or running royalty rates or some combination of these.

Essentially, what you want to do is look at comparables. Comparables are deals involving technology similar to yours or having functionally equivalent importance for end products in your field(s) of use. Then adjust the "fair market royalty rate"—called the industry average royalty rate—to address the specifics of your technology.

Ironically, only you know the real value of the technology because you are the one who is going to use it in your business. Think about the impact it will have on your net revenues and costs of goods sold. Whatever the bump in gross profit you anticipate is the basis for the value of the technology and associated IP. Once you have a guess at this number, you can use some simple math to calculate the value on a net sales basis if that is the way your industry calculates fees and royalty rates.

If you paid out that entire percentage of gross profit to acquire the technology and IP rights, there would be no bottom-line benefit to you for bringing the technology in and turning it into a product (or part of a product or a better way to make a product). So whatever the value you come up with, it is too high to pay for the technology or IP. That value has to be split between you and the other party. This is where comparables come in. If you can get a feel of what people think is reasonable, when you are selling, you want to ask for a price a bit above it and during negotiations come down into the high side of the reasonable range. If you are buying, the reverse holds true. You want to offer a price below the low end of the reasonable range and during negotiations, come up into the low side of the range.

Always remember there is a glut of technology on the market. If you are negotiating with a public entity, point out that a lot of universities, government labs, and other public institutions are offering their technology at no cost or bargain basement prices. That is, after all, why they have nonprofit status. They are supposed to do public good and do not pay taxes because they are not income maximizing like a for-profit. Negotiate hard to see what you can get, but in doing so, be realistic about what the reasonable range is. When you get the best deal you think you can, sign on the dotted line if you feel the price is fair. Fair means you can make a healthy profit if you bring this technology to market even after subtracting the costs of developing, making, selling, and supporting the products that embody it or use it. If you do not like the price, or do not think you can get to a "fair" price, explain what your bottom line is and why you need it. If there still is no deal, walk away. Always remember, there is a lot of technology out there and more is disclosed every day. To quote the song, "It's a small world after all."

Open innovation helps you with products in two ways in this scenario. It provides solutions when you are stumped and it provides products and product enhancements you might never have thought of. That builds revenues. If you manage the process like you would any other important business activity, it also can cut costs in getting products to market. The net result is more profit, which, as agreed earlier, is a good thing.

Recall the second thing that you need to generate more profits is IP rights. At the very least, you need freedom to operate. That means you can make and sell your product and people can use it without worrying about infringement lawsuits. There are all sorts of ways to get this ability. One way is to check what has already been disclosed and thus cannot be protected by anyone. Then, buy at least nonexclusive rights to the technology you absolutely must have for your product and which is not in the unprotected set of technology you just identified.

If you want the exclusive right to some product turf, it probably will cost more because you need to buy a portfolio of IP rights that stakes out a "technology space" broad enough for (1) warding off direct attacks for infringement, (2) build-arounds, and (3) new filings that winnow away at your turf.

The good thing about practicing open innovation is that if you know what you are looking for, it is reasonably easy and usually surprisingly affordable to own the IP portfolio you need. (To quote The Rolling Stones, "You can't always get what you want, but if you try sometimes, you just might find that you get what you need.")

The first thing to do is describe the capabilities, features, and functionalities you absolutely need for freedom to operate (or to claim exclusive turf). Write them down as if they were a set of claims for a patent application. Now search the global patent literature and see if anyone has a filing on them. If they do, try to license it. Look online for technology and patents and patent applications being advertised that cover at least one of your claims until you have covered everything you require.

You want to license as many of those as you can afford within the budget set. You at least need one license for each claim that is not already in the public domain. Otherwise, you cannot secure freedom to operate—a bummer if you are sued.

Of course, it probably makes sense to file your own application for the package.

While you are doing all this, keep an eye out for that diamond in the rough everyone is missing. It can be anything from a way to solve your current requirement to something disruptive in your business model but so potentially lucrative you are still thinking about it.

As we have seen, in the legal nuts and bolts sense, buying technology equates to buying IP rights.

Negotiating IP transactions is mostly common sense. Be clear about your "must haves," "nice to haves," and "No Way Buddy!"s. Then negotiate till you have your must haves and no "No Ways." Your "nice to haves" are trading chips. You try to keep as many as possible but you must always remember they are trading chips. The only other crucial trick is to be nice. Try to understand the negotiation from the other folks' perspective. If you can come up with terms that work for both you and them, there will be a deal. If not, there is not one. This consensus is easier to reach if you see each other as playing on the same team.

That is how you make money at open innovation. You acquire new technology and IP rights to it, turn the technology into one or more products. You sell the products to customers or the IP rights to licensees, or you do both. Open innovation is important for the first and last step of these three steps. The rule of thumb is the same as in any market transaction: Buy low and sell high.

And yes, like every rule, this one has exceptions. The most important one is "Get what you can when you sell off surplus IP." Surplus IP may be technology you just never are going to use.

Surplus IP arises in a variety of ways. Here are three examples. In each case, any revenue you gain, so long as it is higher than the transaction costs of doing the deal, increases your profitability because the cost of acquiring the technology and maintaining its IP protection are sunk costs.

You buy a portfolio. To get the technology or IP you really wanted at a good price, you never disclosed that all you really wanted was a particular part of the portfolio because you were afraid if you did that, the price would jump. So you let them think you were buying their junk for use as trading chips in case you got sued for infringement. If you get sued, hopefully in all that junk is something the party suing you is infringing. Now you can countersue that party and ultimately everyone settles because these lawsuits create a situation where no one is the clear victor. The theory behind the tactic is: If you throw enough, sooner or later something might stick. You can sell non-exclusive rights to the trading chips if you need them, or sell all your rights if you do not need them.

You only care about exclusive rights in your field of use, but to get an exclusive license in your field, you had to take an across-the-board exclusive license. The reason the seller wants you to take the all-encompassing exclusive is that it is normal in IP deals for the burden of paying patent or other IP maintenance fees passes from the licensor to the licensee. In non-exclusive or more limited licenses, the licensee typically is still obligated to pay the maintenance fees. If you can sell sublicenses to noncompeting companies for noncompeting uses, it reduces the cost of acquisition and may even turn a profit itself.

The technology is old and you have moved on to new technological platforms. No harm in selling or licensing that IP as whatever you get is gravy.

Open innovation is helpful when selling surplus IP, just as it is when buying and selling IP more important for your company. You can use crowdsourcing, brokers, auctions, and so on, or even set up your own out-licensing unit to sell it (i.e., set up your own technology transfer office).

So we conclude as we began: Open innovation is a way to make more profit. There are lots of opportunities for that right now. It looks like there will be solid opportunities for SMEs for at least the next decade. Hopefully this book has helped you figure out how to grab your piece of the pie.

Index

OTHER TITLES IN THE ENTREPRENEURSHIP AND SMALL BUSINESS MANAGEMENT COLLECTION

Scott Shane, Case Western University, Editor

- *The Chinese Entrepreneurship Way: A Case Study Approach* by Julia Pérez-Cerezo
- *Enhancing the Managerial DNA of Your Small Business* by Pat Roberson-Saunders, Barron H. Harvey, Philip Fanara, Jr., Gwynette P. Lacy and Pravat Choudhury
- *Five Eyes on the Fence: Protecting the Five Core Capitals of Your Business* by Tony A. Rose
- *Hispanic–Latino Entrepreneurship: Viewpoints of Practitioners* by J. Mark Munoz and Michelle Ingram Spain
- *The Business Wealth Builders: Accelerating Business Growth, Maximizing Profits, and Creating Wealth* by Phil Symchych and Alan Weiss

Announcing the Business Expert Press Digital Library

Concise e-books business students need for classroom and research

This book can also be purchased in an e-book collection by your library as

- a one-time purchase,
- that is owned forever,
- allows for simultaneous readers,
- has no restrictions on printing, and
- can be downloaded as PDFs from within the library community.

Our digital library collections are a great solution to beat the rising cost of textbooks. E-books can be loaded into their course management systems or onto students' e-book readers.
The **Business Expert Press** digital libraries are very affordable, with no obligation to buy in future years. For more information, please visit **www.businessexpertpress.com/librarians**. To set up a trial in the United States, please email **sales@businessexpertpress.com**.

www.ingramcontent.com/pod-product-compliance
Lightning Source LLC
Chambersburg PA
CBHW050106210326
41519CB00015BA/3848